3d drawing and optical illusions

How to draw optical illusions and 3d art step by step Guide for Kids, Teens and Students

New edition

Sophia Williams

TABLE OF CONTENTS

How to use the book, How does it work? - 3

How to draw your own 3D drawings on paper - 4

Tips for beginners - 5

Hole in hand - 6

2 pits - 10

Card deck - 14

Pencil - 18

The letter "A" - 20

Hole - 24

Ghost - 28

Plane - 32

Flying figures - 35

Flying heart - 38

More from Sophia Williams - 41

HOW TO USE THE BOOK

This book contains step-by-step instructions and detailed examples for drawing 3D drawings. Read the instructions and look at the graphic examples to accurately repeat the pictures. Most photos contain tools (pencil, ruler, and eraser) that you need to use for the specific drawing. Instructions and examples are written in such a way that you can create a beautiful drawing without skills. But if you did not succeed in repeating the drawing the first time, don't be discouraged, sometimes even professionals fail. Just try again, taking into account the mistakes made.

HOW DOES IT WORK?

3D drawings create the illusion of a three-dimensional shape. How is it achieved? With the help of volume. To give volume to drawn and colored objects, artists use their skills with shadows and shading.

If you put an object on the table and install a light source on the side, you'll see that the spot located closer to the light has glare. And the farther the subject from the light source, the darker it becomes. It also casts its own shadow. The effect of these drawings lies in the correct rendering of shadows. But if you look at your subject from another point of view and then the place where the glare is formed, as well as where the dimming occurs, the object's own shadow can change. Therefore, three-dimensional drawings have only a single point from which they look natural.

HOW TO DRAW YOUR OWN 3D DRAWINGS ON PAPER

The first step is to create a sketch of the drawing. Make a clear plan on which objects will be placed on the page where, for each subject, a specific place will be allocated and a certain shape will be given. Determine the location of the light source in relation to the objects. This is necessary in order to create the shadow correctly.

Objects close to the light source should be brighter than those that are farther away.

The second stage is drawing the shadows. Drawing shadows is best done in layers; that is, first draw light sketches of the shadow, and then then darken them with new layers.

The choice of pencil is very important. The softer the pencil, the easier it is to create a shadow. Additionally, the structure of the paper also matters. For your art experiments, thick, white, glossy paper is the best choice.

In order for the picture to look as realistic as possible, the shadow itself must have fuzzy, blurry outlines.

TIPS FOR BEGINNERS

Always start drawing with a pencil. It can always be erased.

In order to draw a picture you have created, lock your phone or camera in one position. View it and draw only from this angle.

If you want to show off the picture to your friends, it's best to take a photo from the best point of view you can find to demonstrate the 3D effect. If you are showing a drawing, then someone may view it from an unideal vantage point and not see an optical illusion.

To make the shadow look more realistic, rub it with your finger or a dry, clean cloth.

Try to create a pattern from left to right (if you're right-handed), and from top to bottom, so you cannot blur the picture with the lower side of the palm. If you still have to correct something and the palm of your hand might touch the finished drawing, put a clean piece of paper under your hand.

HOLE IN HAND

1. Take 2 sheets with a similar or identical text.
2. On one of them, draw a circle. Use a round object to get an exact trace. Don't forget that the circle shouldn't be very larger than the palm of your hand.
3. Carefully cut out the circle.
4. On the top, draw an arc (as shown on the picture).
5. Color the arc in red.
6. Add a shadow from the upper side by coloring a little less than half of the arc.
7. Now make a shadow from the bottom. The bottom outline should be almost black. The farther the shadow is from the outline, the lighter it should be.
8. Put the circle on your palm and dot 5–6 points around the perimeter.
9. Circle the dots with a red felt tip pen to make a circle in the palm of your hand. The circle in the palm of your hand should be slightly larger than the paper circle.
10. Place the paper circle on the circle in the palm of your hand and place your hand over the second sheet of text.

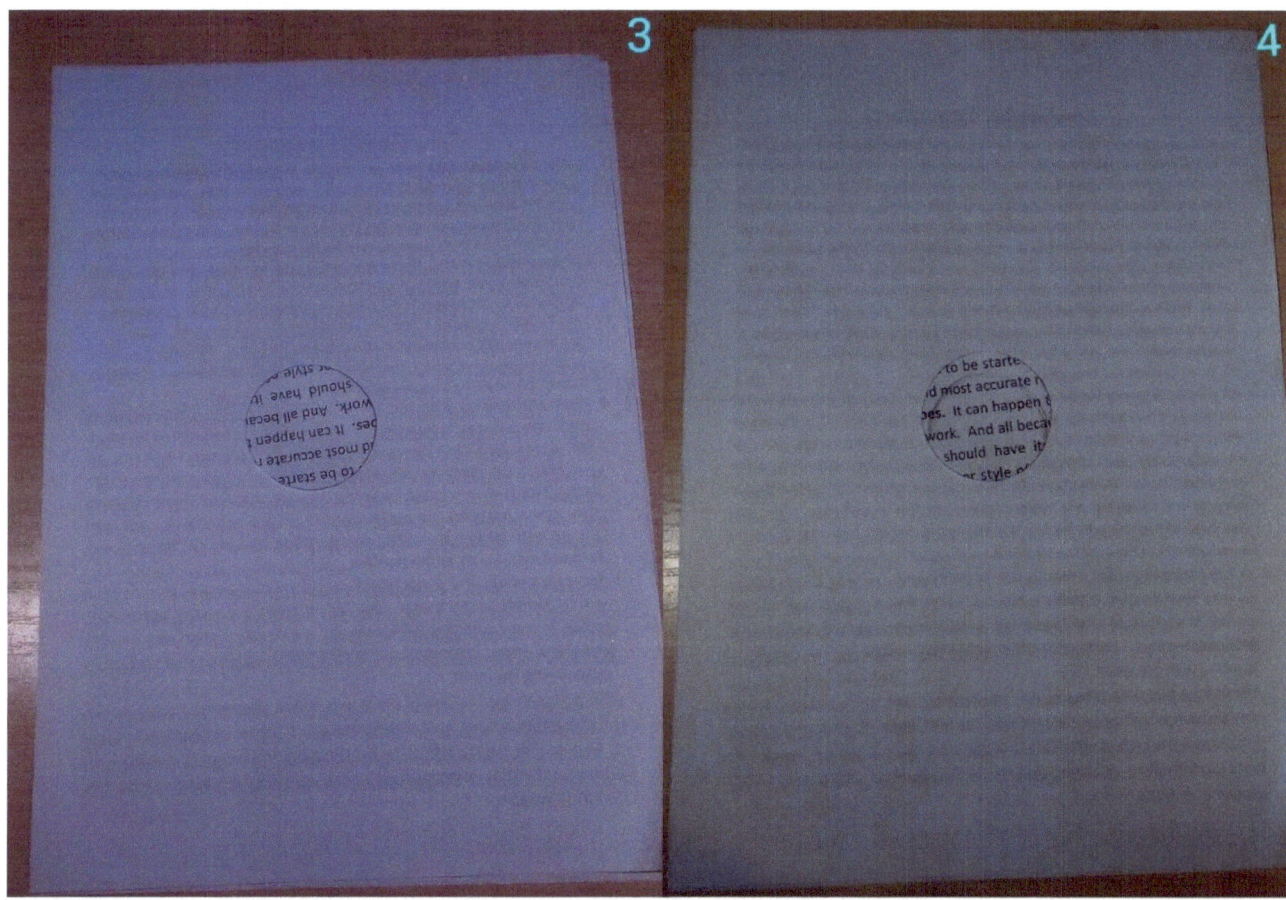

Tips for beginners:

1. **The proportions of the body.** In the anime, the body of the characters is built so that it somehow reflects their mood. Improve your skills, and this will give you the opportunity to create completely different proportions. As a result, you may find your own style. Look at any anime comic, and you will see how the shape of the body changes, even for the same hero.
2. **From sketch to detail.** Always start with a sketch and only then gradually fill the drawing with details. If you start to draw complex glare on your eyes, without even finishing drawing your face, it may end up so that the eye isn't at all where it is needed, and you will have to erase everything. Never leave the noticed errors unattended, even if their correction will require a lot of time, or even if everything has to be started anew! Guidelines and sketches help you achieve the best and most accurate result.
3. **Distinctive features of heroes.** It can happen to every comic book artist that readers lose interest in his work. And all because they find all the characters too similar. Each character should have its own distinctive features, for example, in hair, eyes, growth, or style of clothing (unless, according to the author's idea, everything should be the other way around). Think in advance what colors, hairstyles, and accessories will suit this or that hero. Also, you can beat the picture by adding an interesting background, the elements surrounding the hero, or the storyline.
4. **Focus on a mirror.** Put a small mirror in front of your picture. This is a great way to identify your mistakes. You will notice that a sketch that seemed perfect to you actually has flaws, such as, for example, crooked eyes or other anatomical errors. Continue to work on the image until you are completely satisfied with the result.
5. **The female body.** The lines of the female body in the anime are usually very smooth and reflect the ideal of female beauty in Japan. Pronounced muscles or Amazon girls are less attractive, and therefore less common. However, the technique of adding magnificent breasts to distinguish an adult girl from a GIRL IS VERY COMMON.

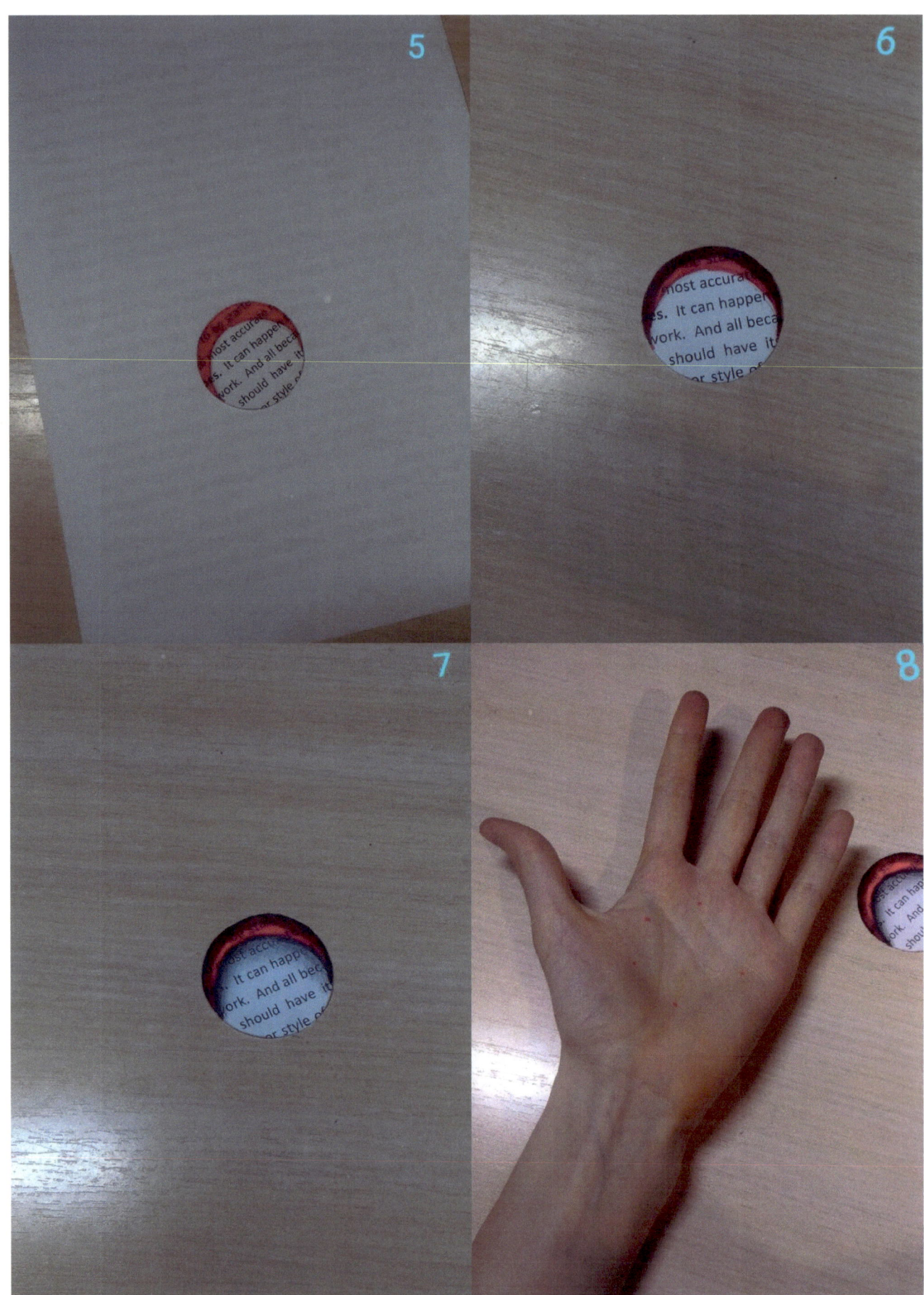

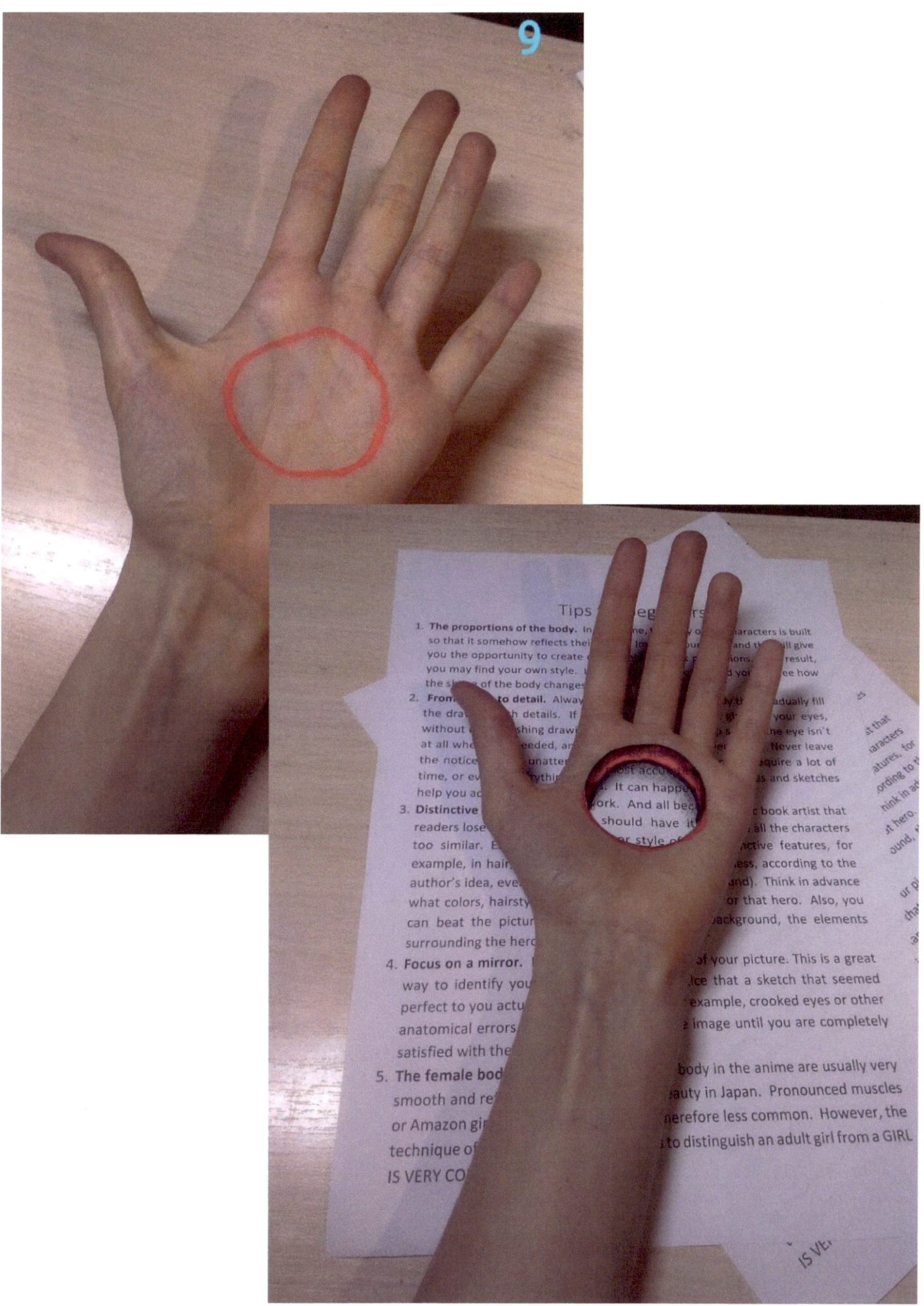

2 PITS

1. Using a pencil draw, 2 identical squares.
2. Draw a line diagonally from the upper right corner to the bottom of the left side. The line should rest against the left wall and not the left corner!
3. Draw horizontal and vertical lines. They should be at equal distances in both squares.
4. In the right square, draw the bricks (use a ruler to make the lines even).
5. Now all lines can be circled with a pen or felt tip pen.
6. Flip the pattern over and shade in the shadow. The upper right corners don't need to be shaded.
7. Done. Look at the picture from the same angle.

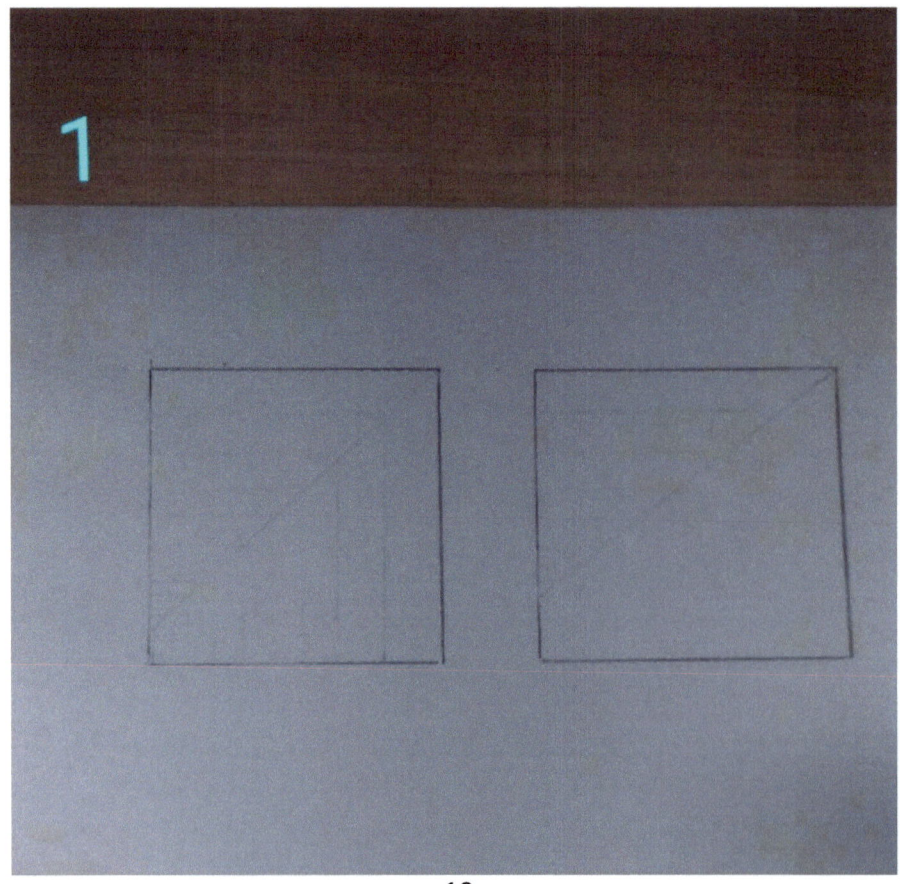

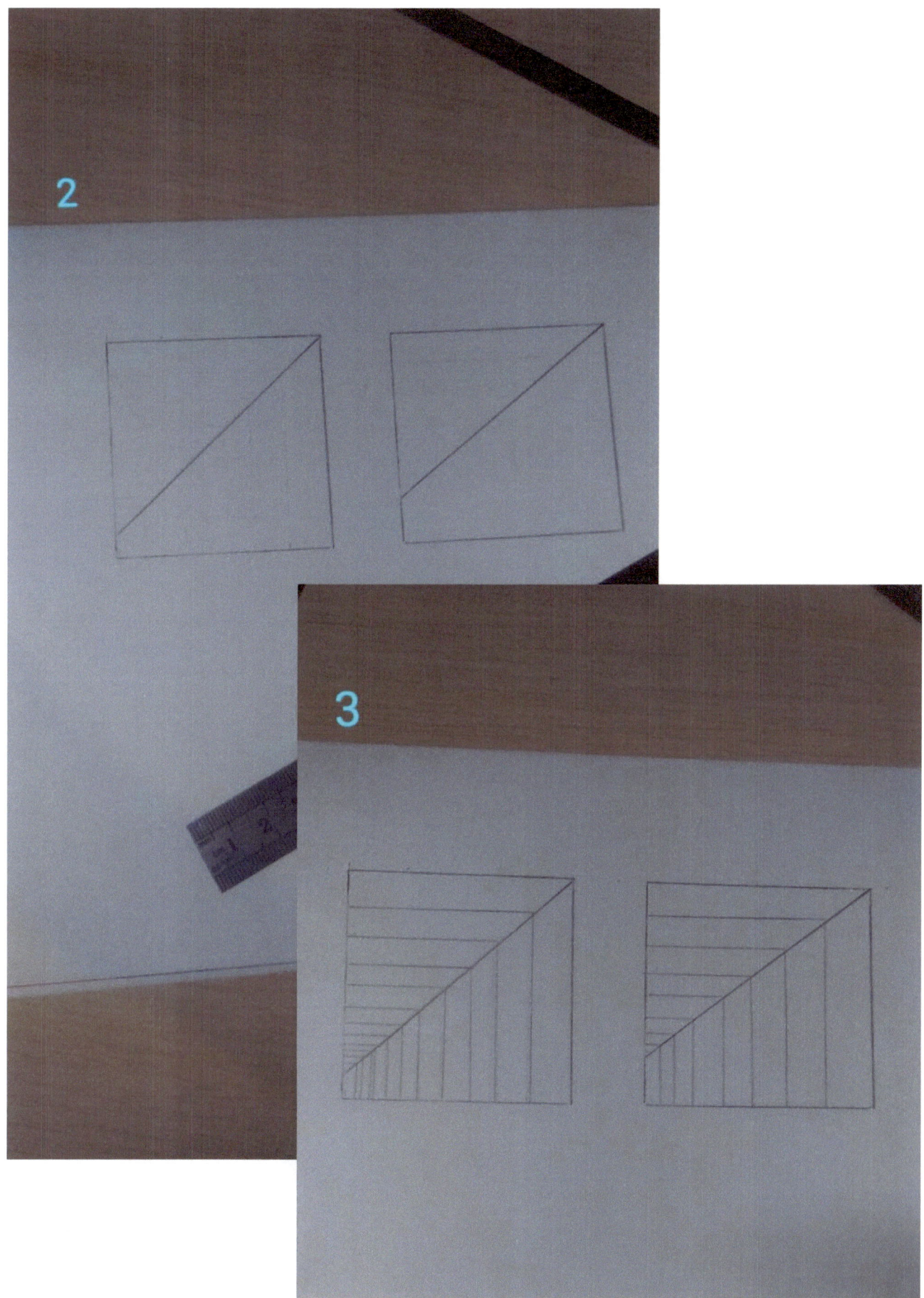

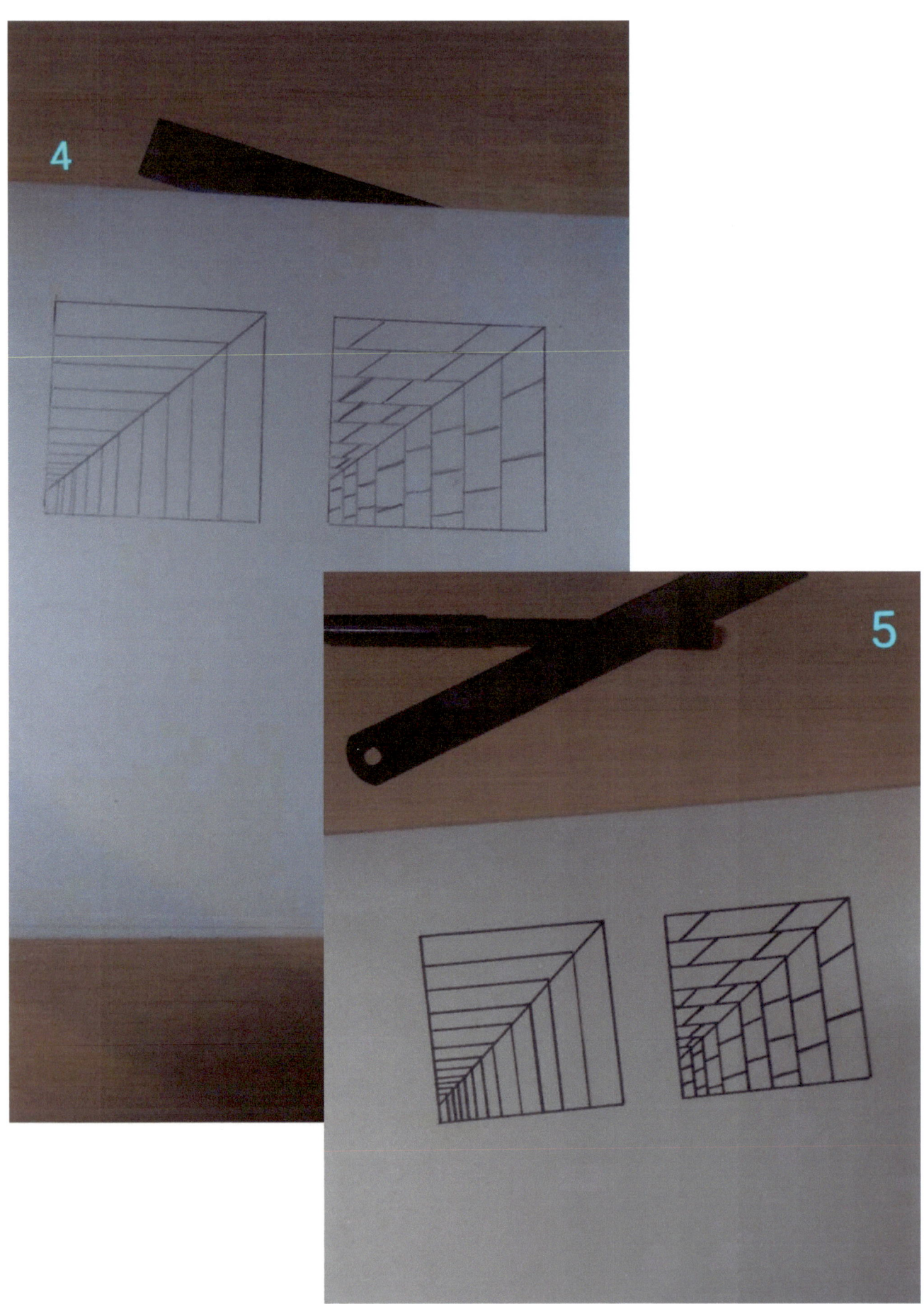

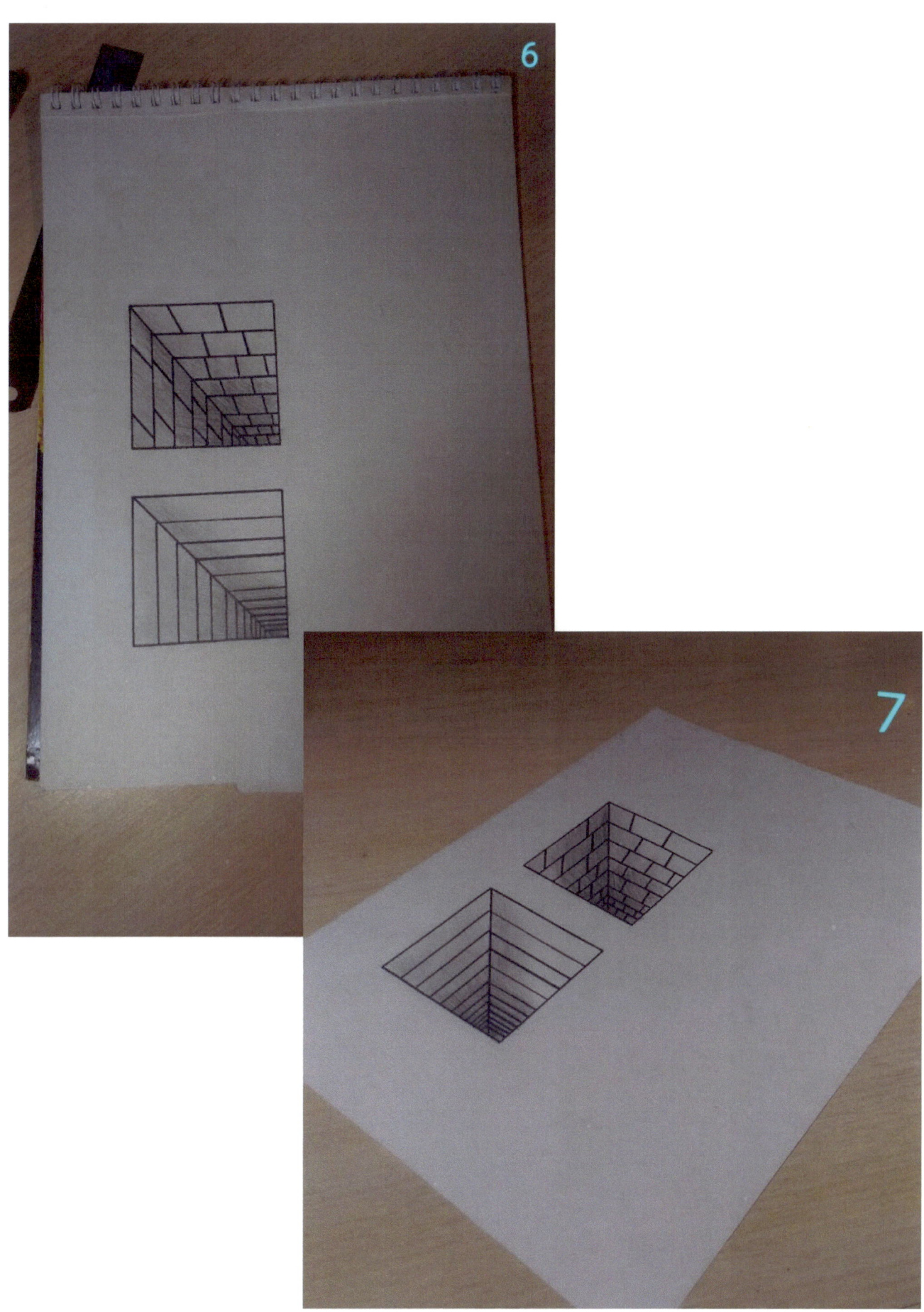

CARD DECK

1. Place a card to the left edge of the sheet. It should be located just above the middle.
2. Outline the shape.
3. Draw the suit and number from the card on it.
4. Color the image and add volume to the deck. 2 corners should be rounded.
5. Using a ruler, draw lines on the sides.
6. Draw the corner with rounded lines.
7. At the beginning and at the end of each side, make a little shadow to add realism.
8. Under the deck, in the same place as in the drawing, draw the first layer of shadow with a pencil. Don't press down hard with the pencil.
9. Rub the resulting shadow with your finger so that it looks uniform and the line from a pencil isn't visible.
10. Now again shade the shadow from the deck, and again rub it with your finger so it becomes much more realistic.
11. As in the figure, mark the lines to be cut out.
12. Cut the pattern.
13. Done. Look at the picture from the same angle.

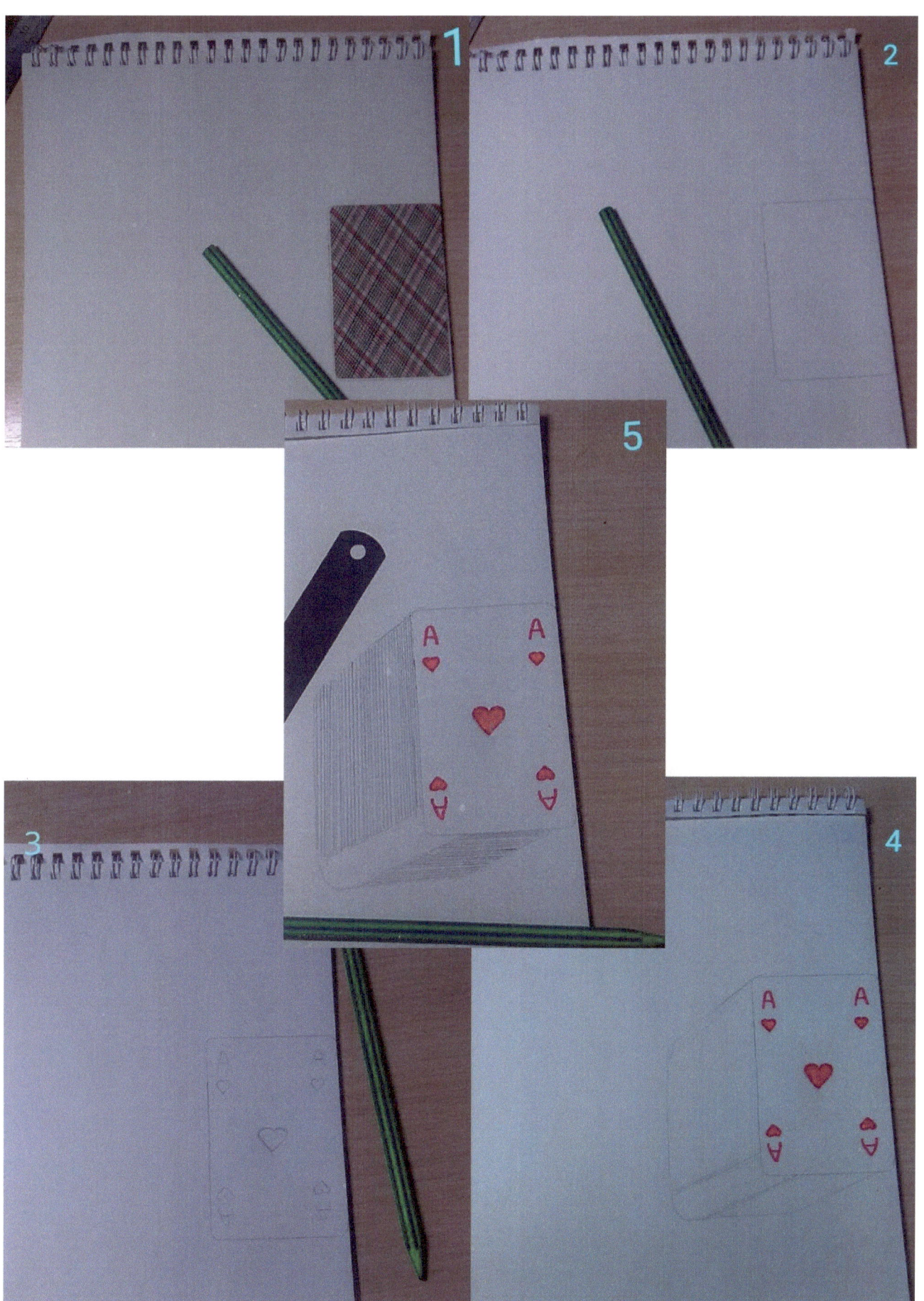

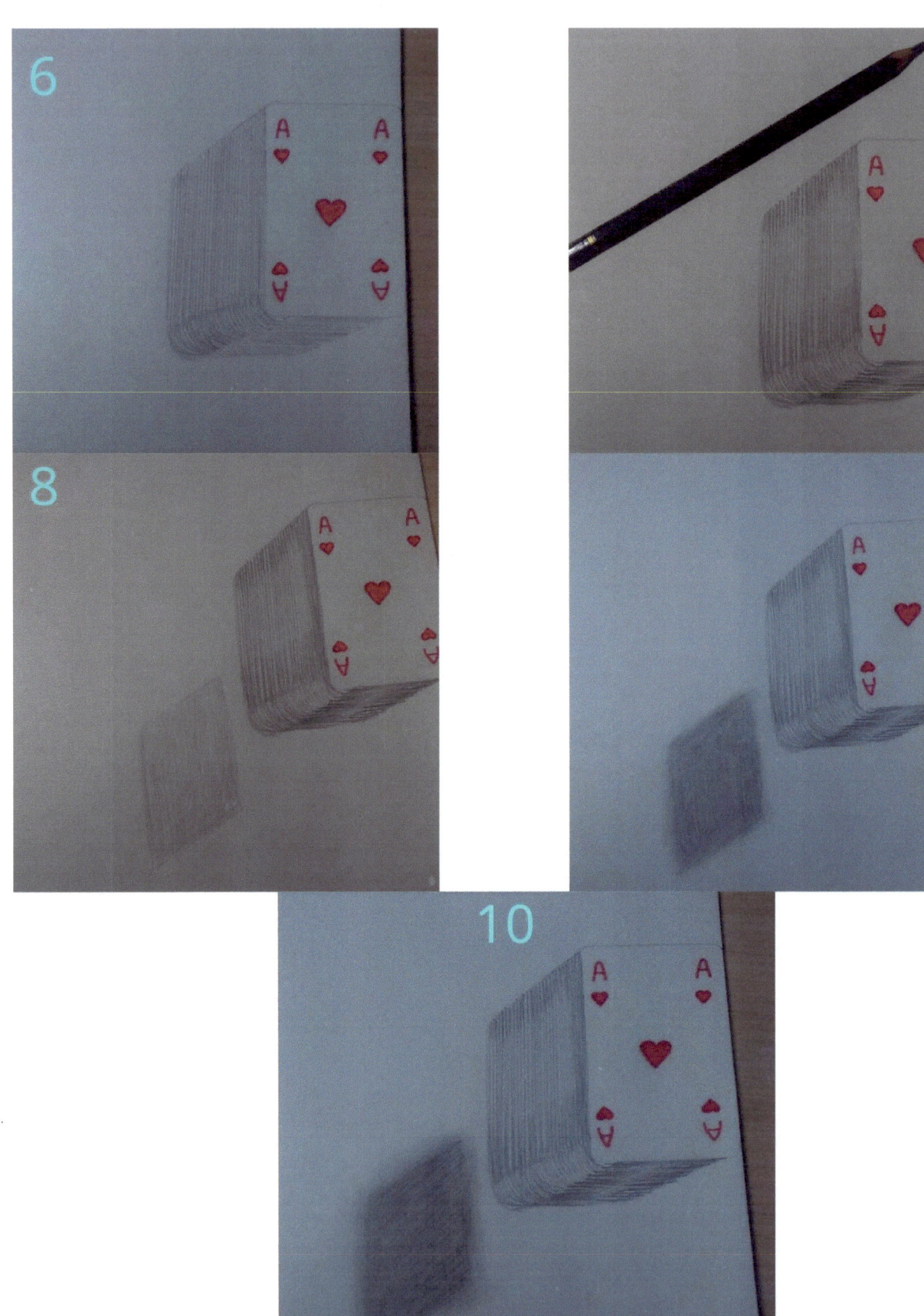

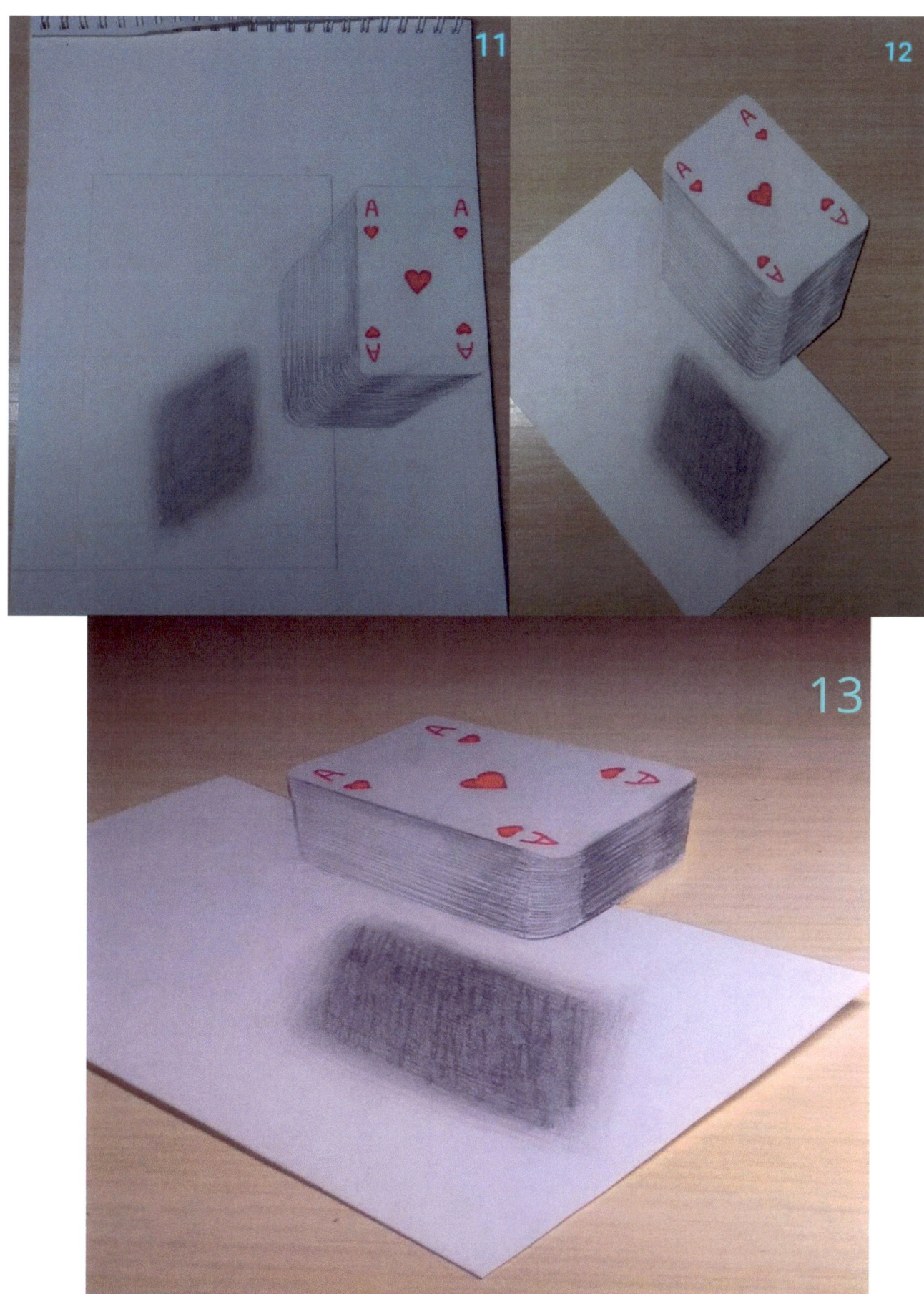

PENCIL

1. In two lines, divide the sheet with a pencil into 4 equal parts. Draw a curved pencil.
2. Draw 3 faces to the pencil.
3. Sketch a shadow. It should be slightly closer to the center of the sheet.
4. Shade the tip of the pencil, then shade the edges. The leftmost edge should be the darkest, the edge in the middle is a bit lighter, and the rightmost side is almost white.
5. Shade in the shadow. For greater realism, the top and bottom of the shadow should be slightly darker than the middle.
6. Erase the lines with which we divided the sheet. Bend the pattern and place it against the wall. Done!

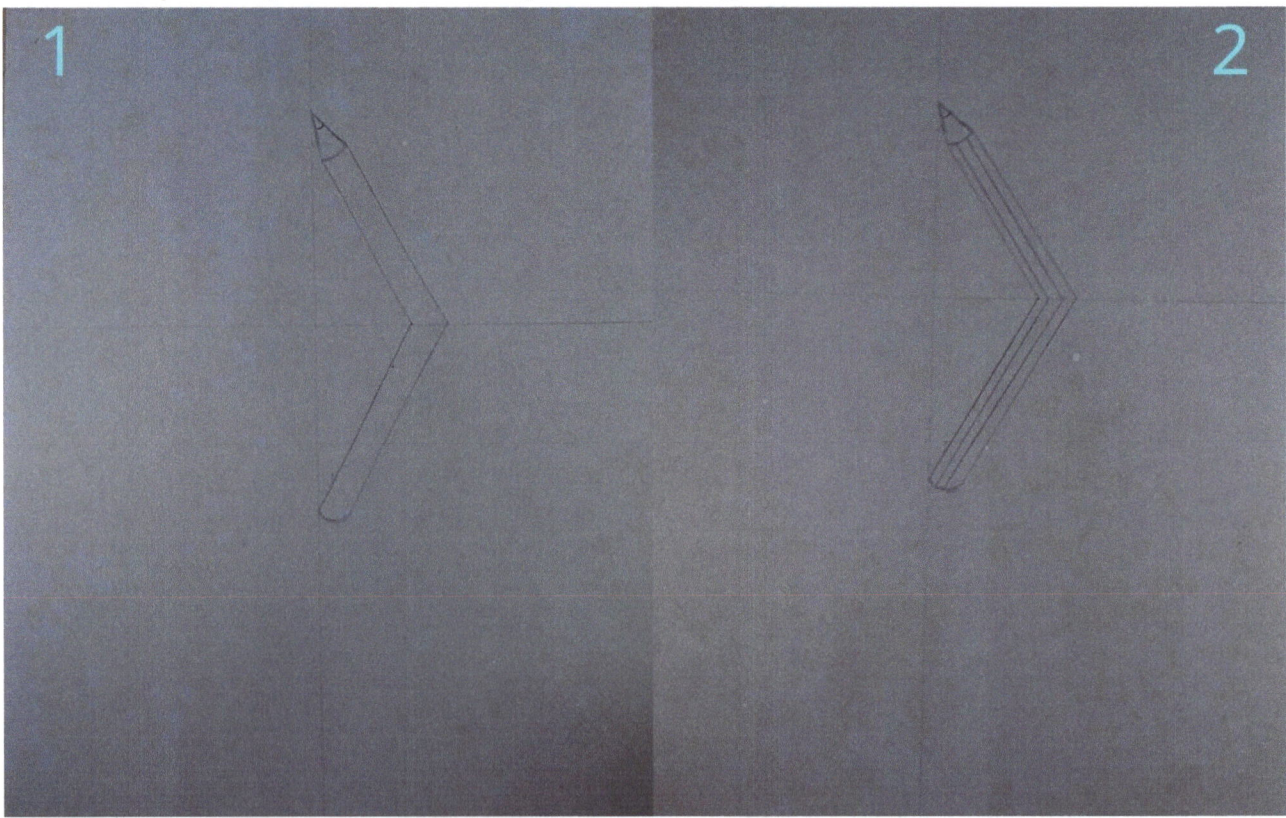

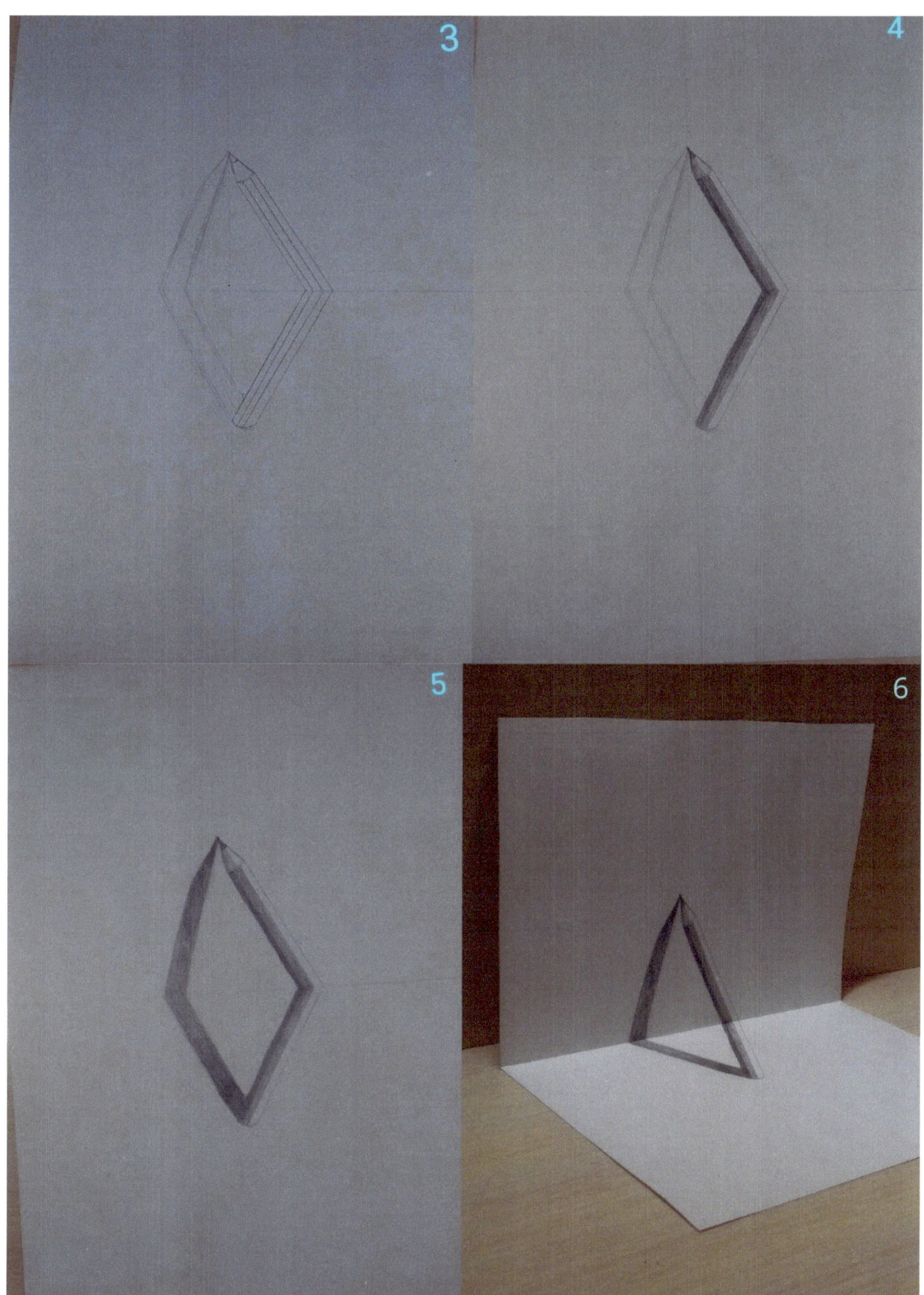

THE LETTER "A"

1. Draw a square that fits easily into your palm.
2. Draw the letter "A" in it.
3. Give the letter volume.
4. Color the volumetric sides and outline with a red felt tip pen.
5. With a pencil, make a shadow as shown in the picture and shade the volumetric sides.
6. Gently cut off the excess.
7. Put the drawing on your hand, and under your hand place a sheet of white paper. Done!

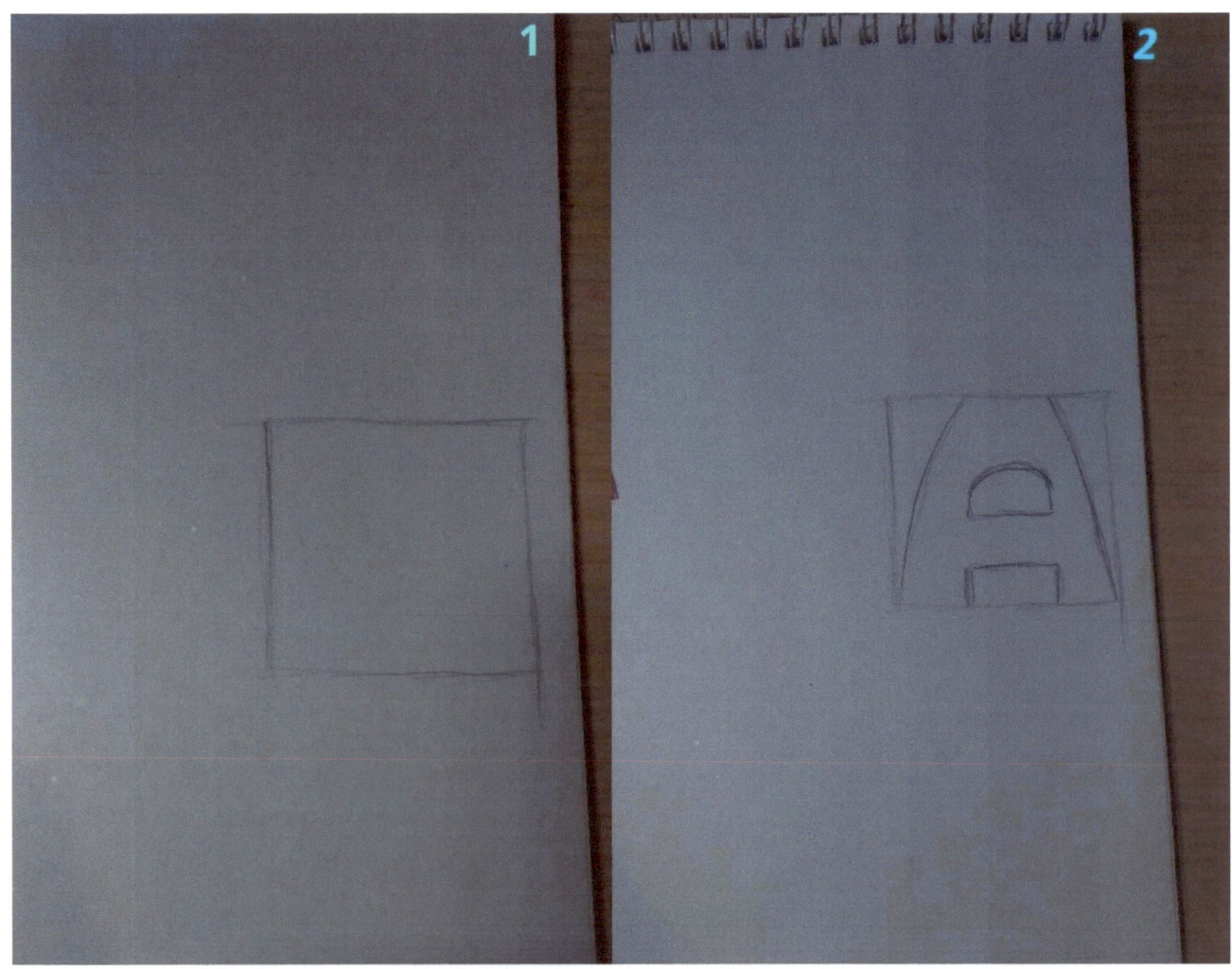

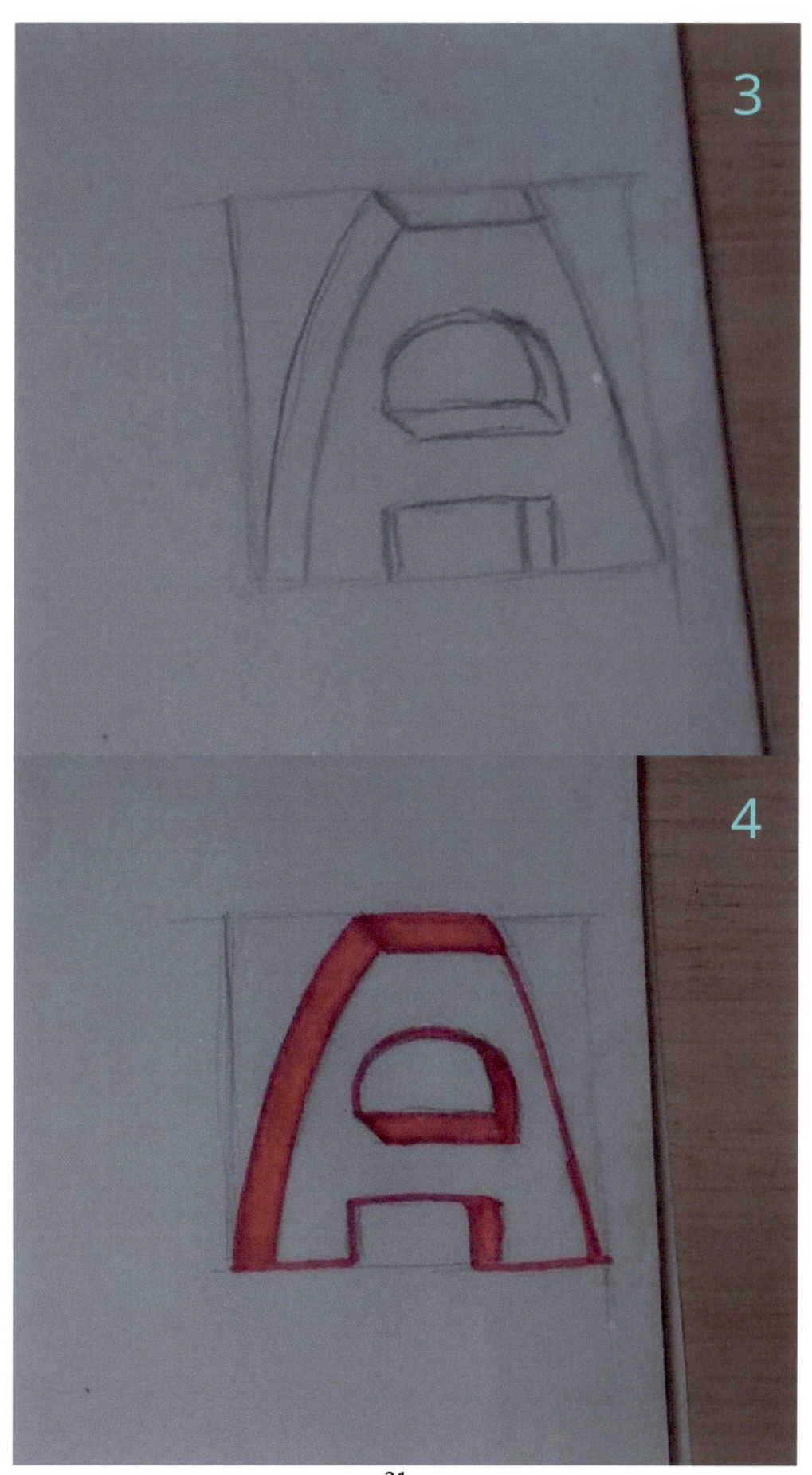

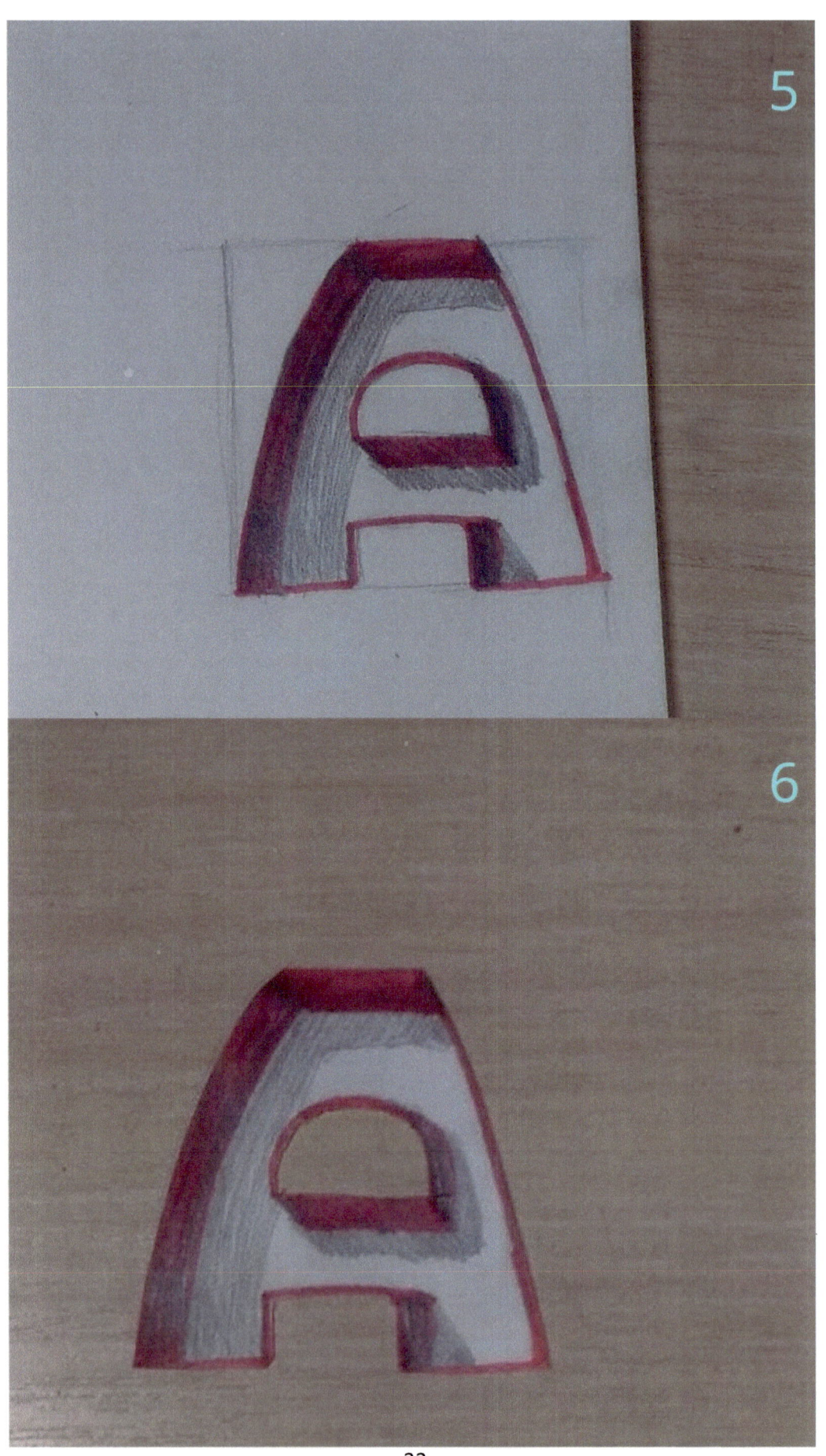

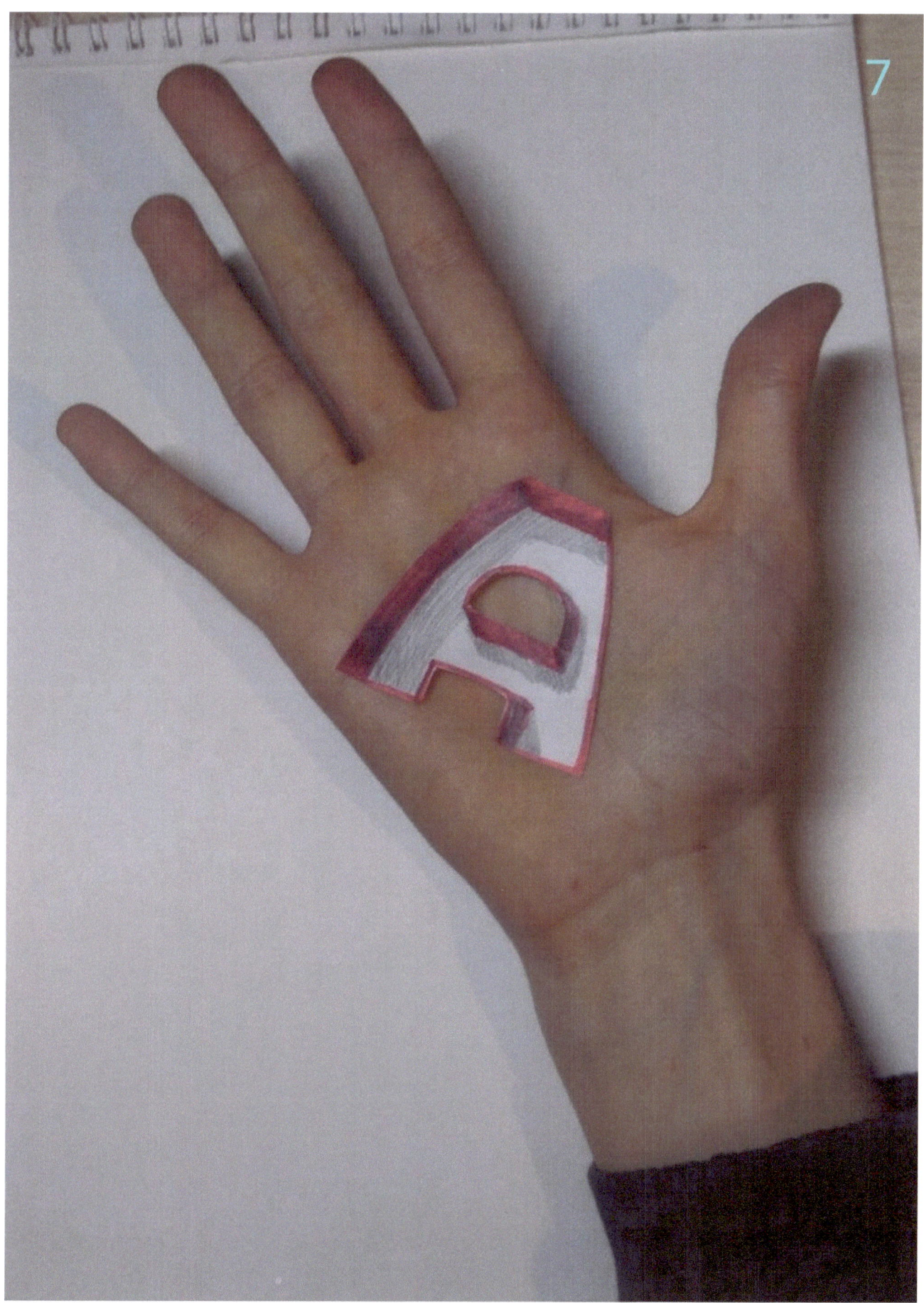

HOLE

1. Make a square sheet and draw 8 equal horizontal lines in pencil.
2. Now draw 8 equal lines vertically. You should get 9x9 identical squares.
3. In the box that you see in the figure, draw the same line from one corner to another.
4. Erase unnecessary lines.
5. Go over all lines with a pen or felt tip pen.
6. Add a shadow to the top side. Don't press down hard with the pencil, as this side should be light.
7. Make a shadow on the second side. This shadow should be a little darker.
8. Color in the bottom with a black felt tip pen.
9. Position the picture in the same way as shown so that the illusion looks as realistic as possible. Done!

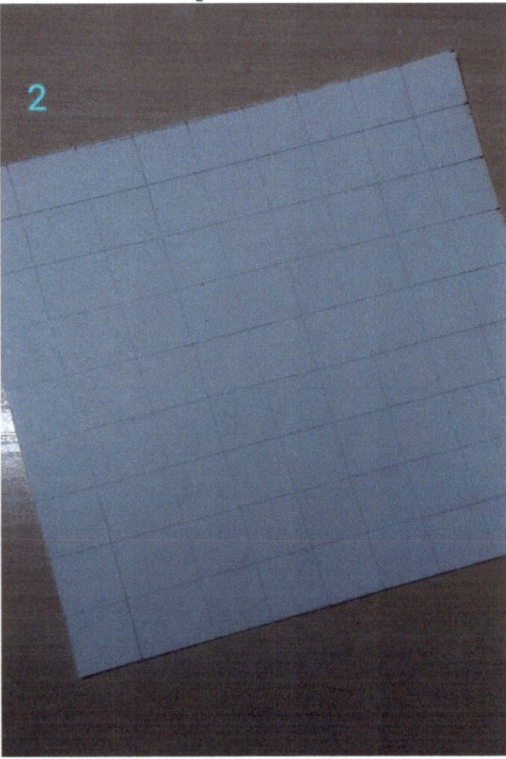

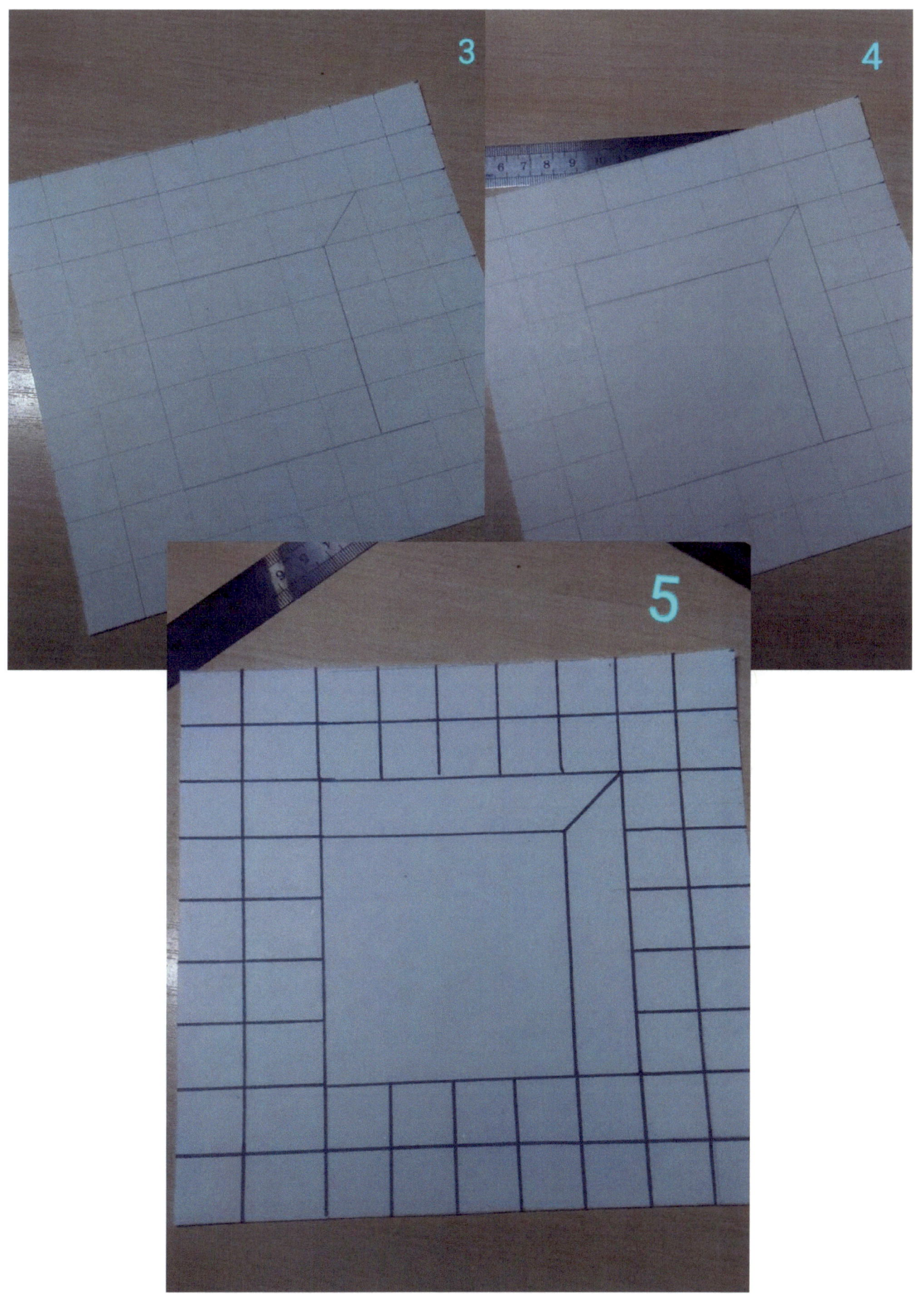

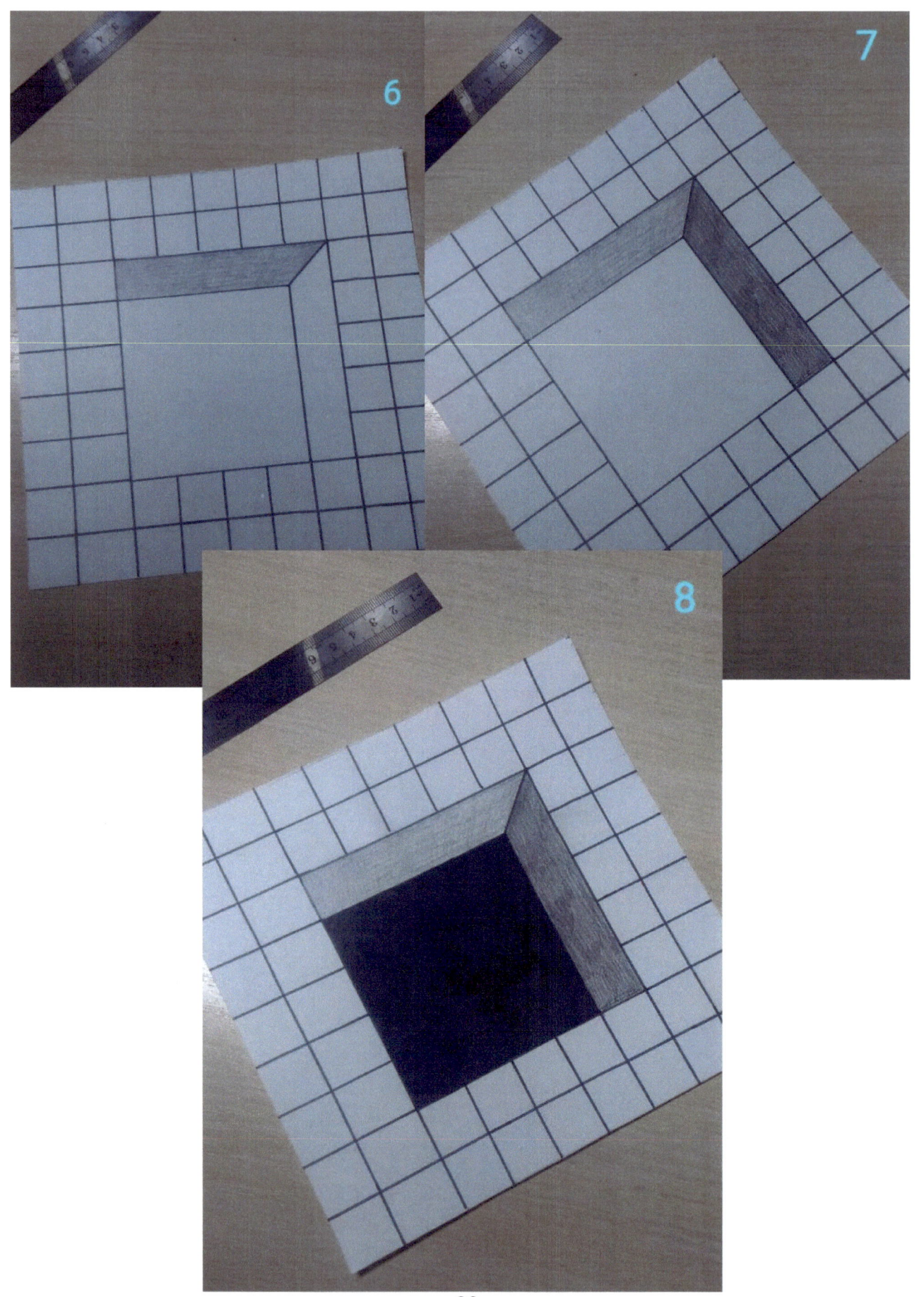

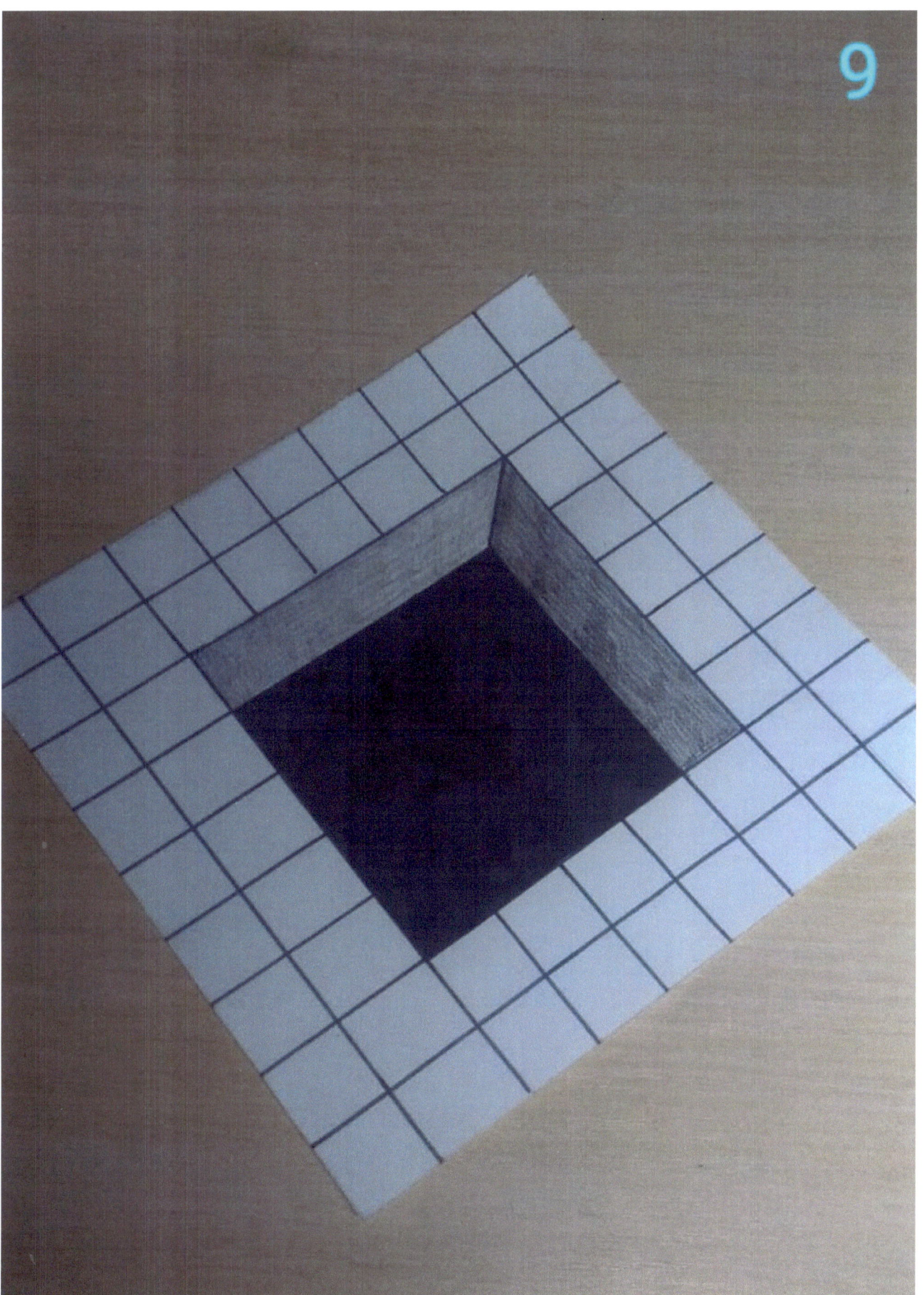

GHOST

1. This is a very complex drawing, so try to follow the instructions as accurately as possible. Take a piece of paper and start drawing from the upper right corner to the lower left. Draw with a pencil so that you can correct errors. Before you start, review at all the steps.

2. When the outline is ready, color in the holes with a felt tip pen.

3. Now you can select the path to trace over the lines.

4. Make a shadow. In our figure, the light source is on the left side, so the shadows will be on the right side. Next, draw a shadow under the cast for greater realism. You can rub it with your finger.

5. Measure the cut lines as shown in the figure.

6. Cut and put at an angle where the picture will look as realistic as possible. Done!

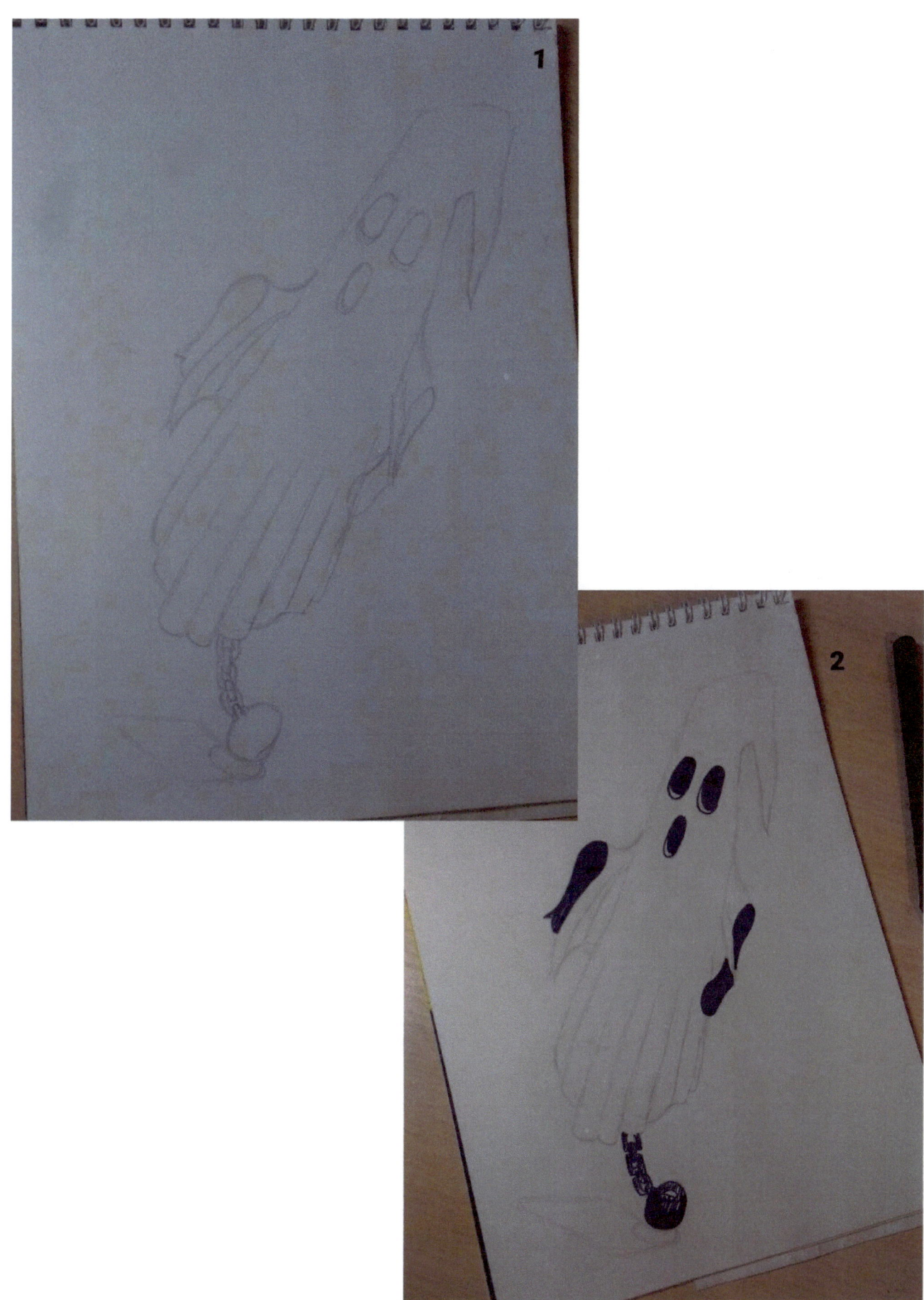

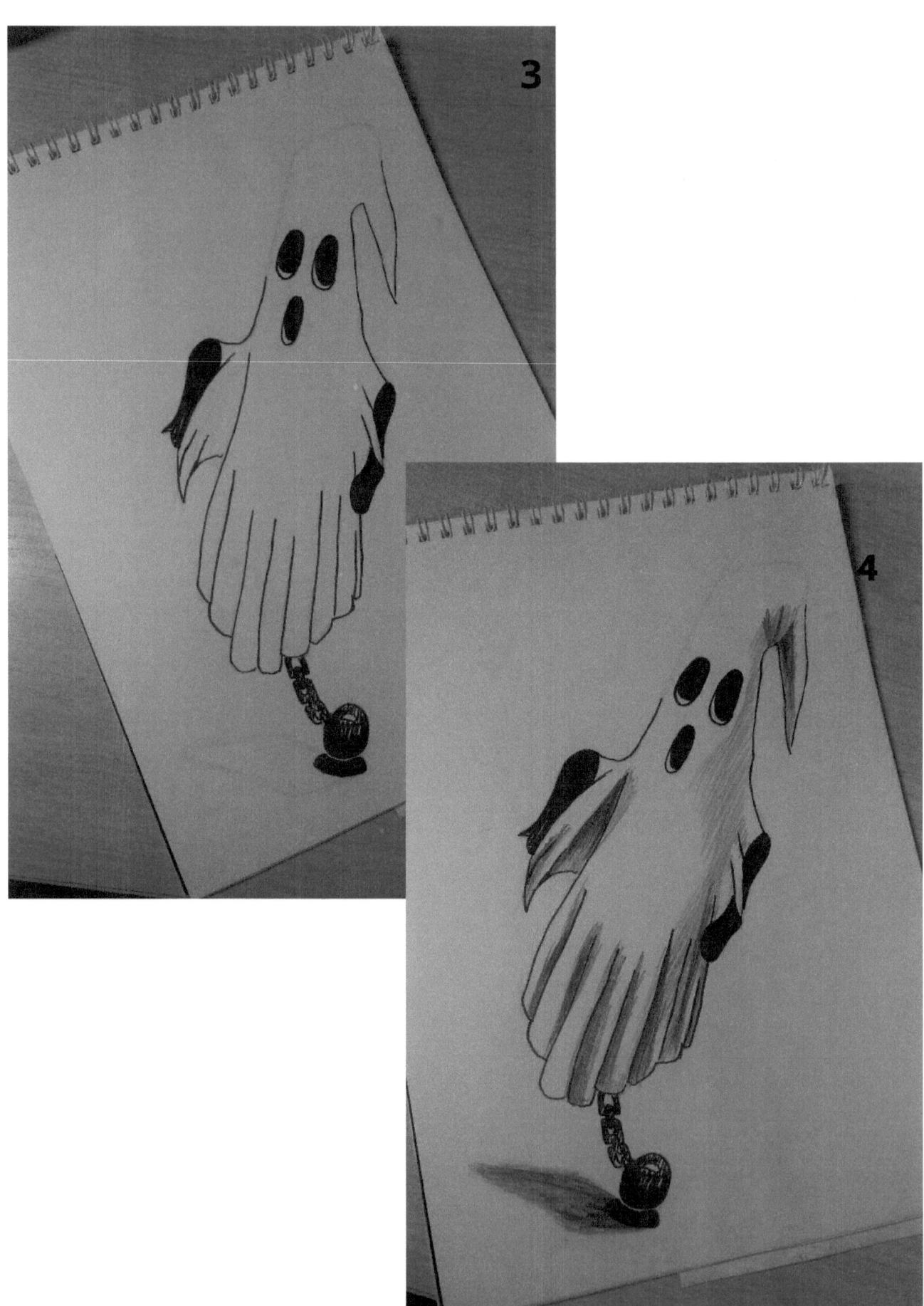

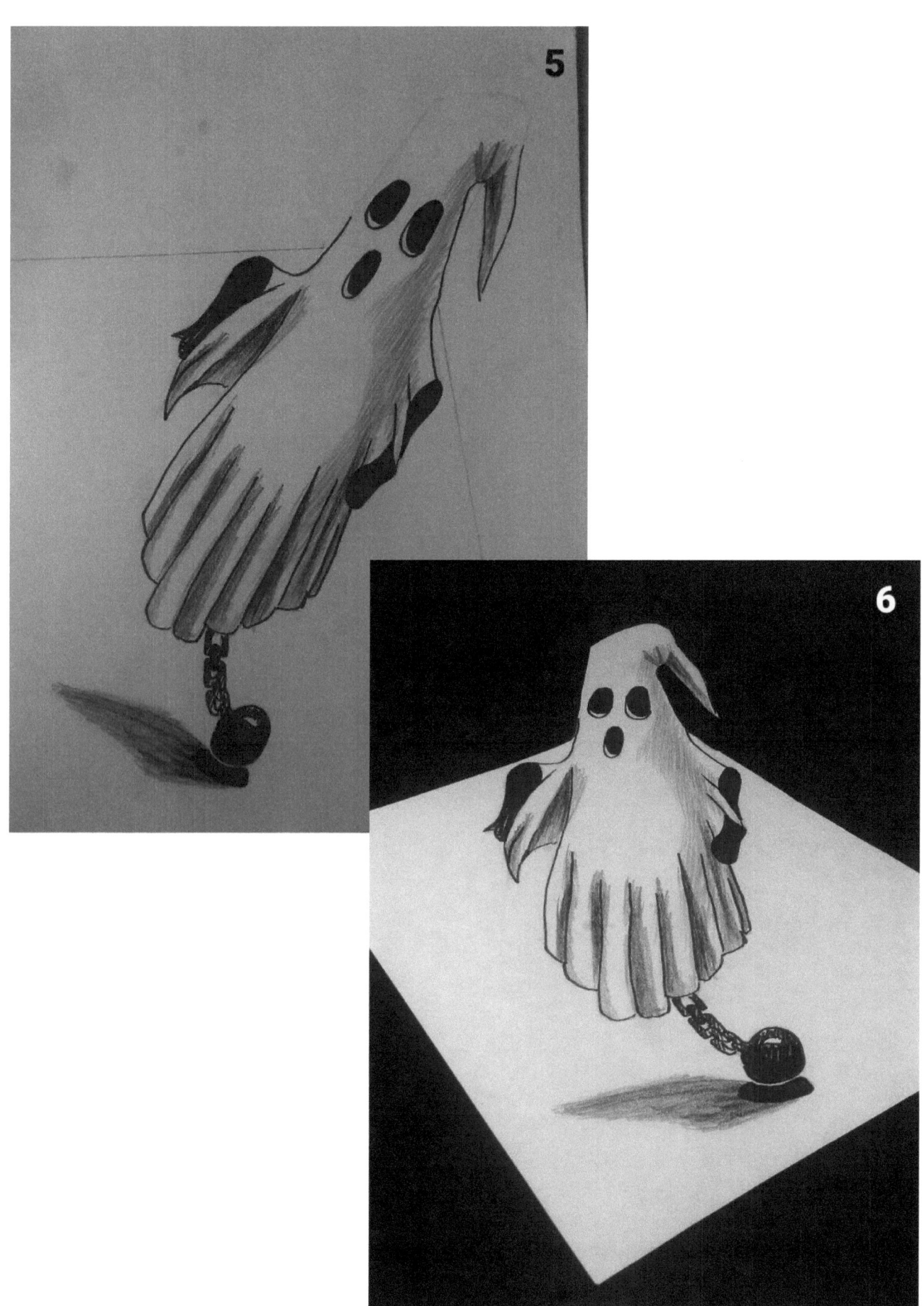

PLANE

1. This is also a complex drawing, so try to follow the instructions as carefully as possible. Review all the steps in advance, and use a pencil first. Draw a plane and outline a shadow under it.

2. Color it in, but not completely, as in the picture. Bright places are glare, like on real airplanes.

3. Make a shadow.

4. Draw the cut lines as shown in the photo.

5. Cut and select the angle at which the picture will look as realistic as possible.

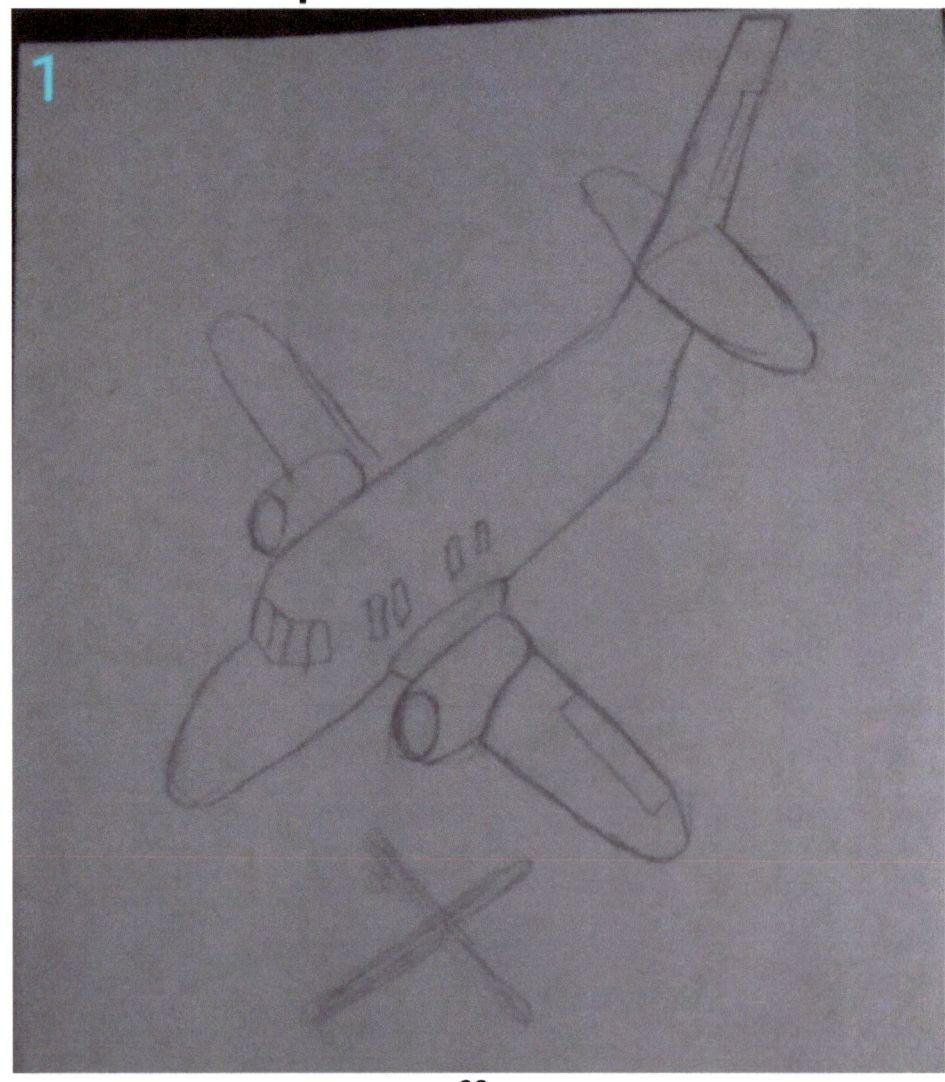

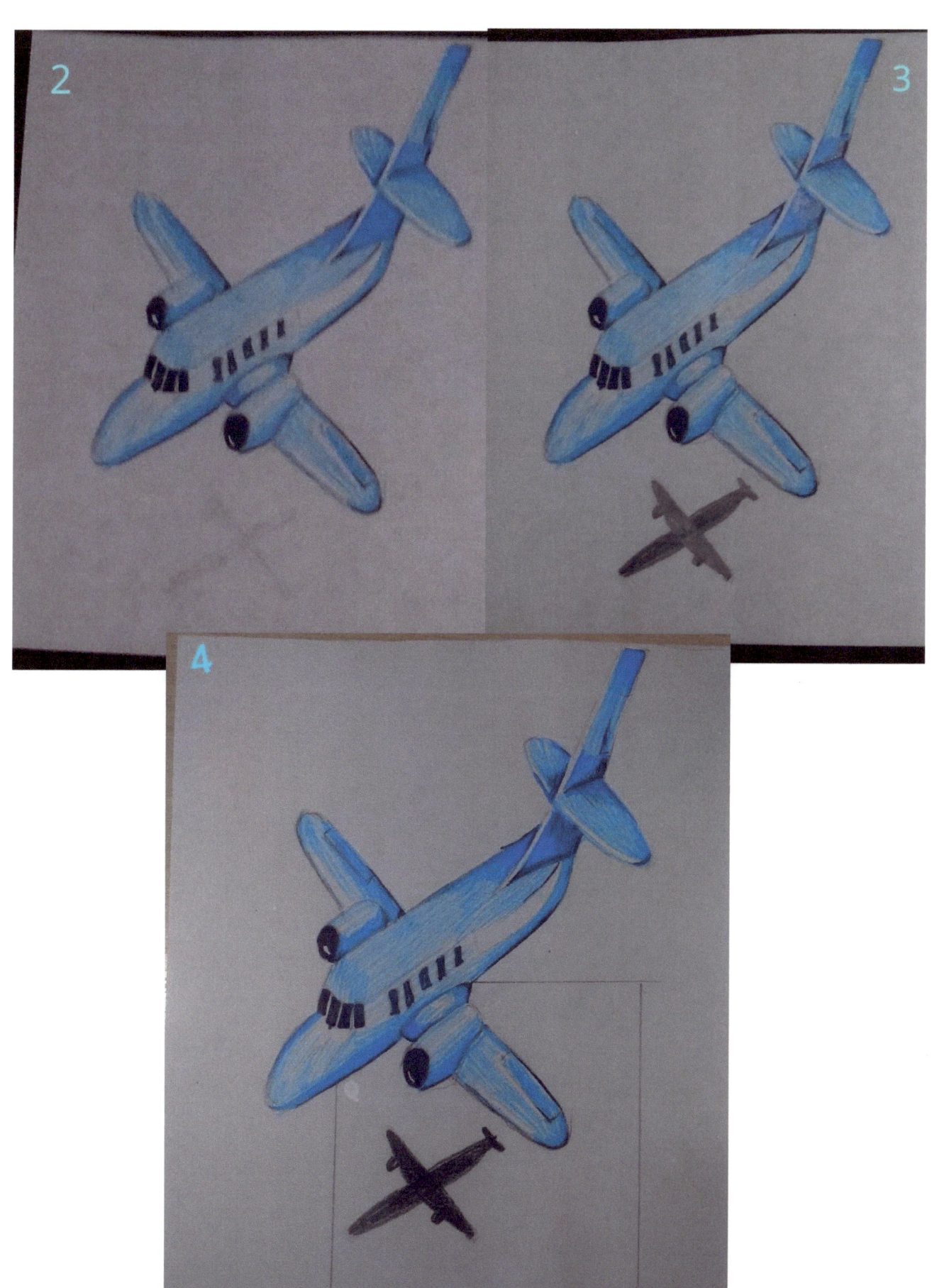

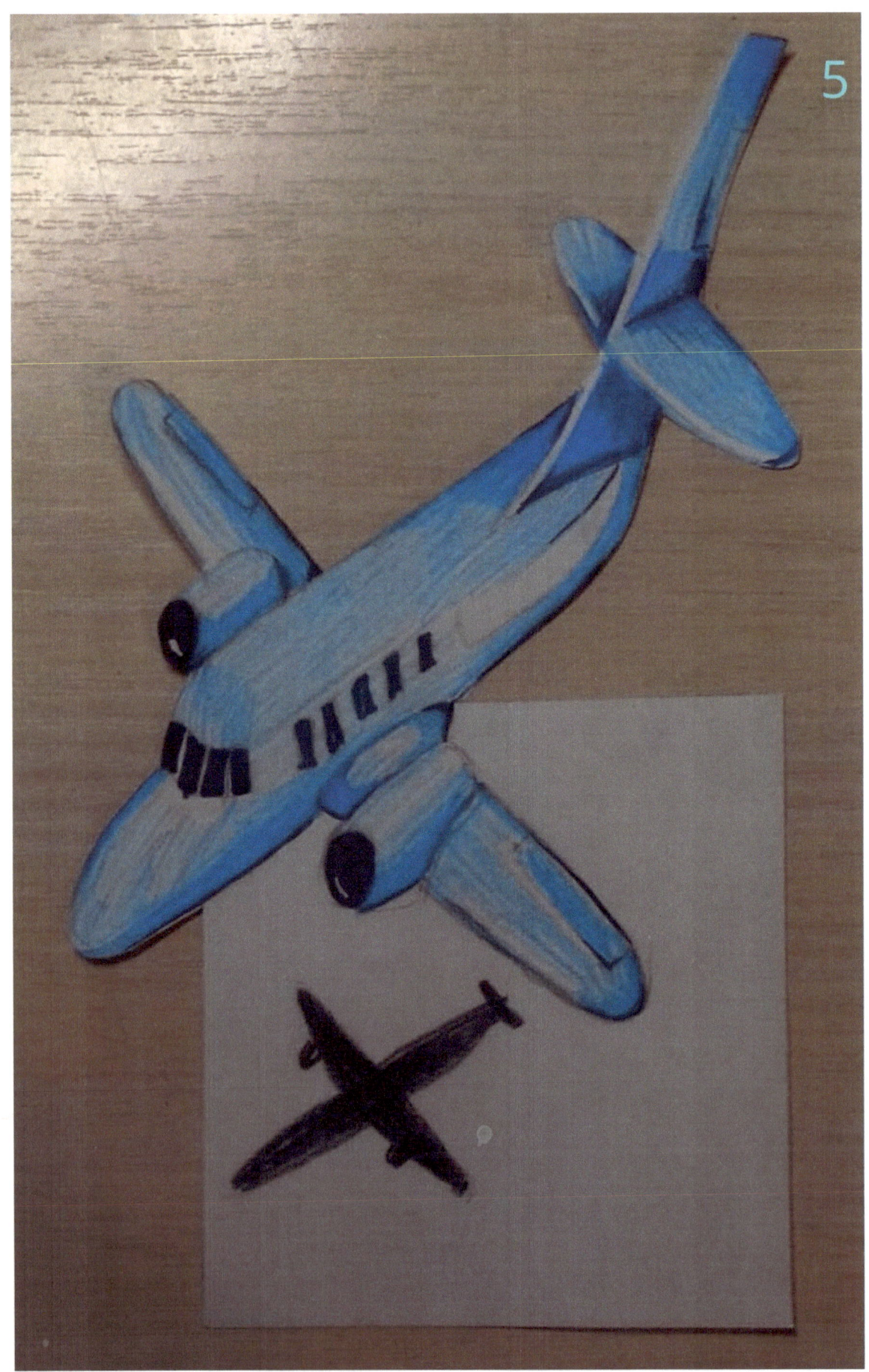

FLYING FIGURES

1. Take 3 pencils in hand . Stack them evenly, one above the other.
2. All 3 pencils at the same time write the number 20.
3. We've made 3 layers. Outline the top layer.
4. Connect the lines of the top layer to the middle layer.
5. Add stroke lines down the number 2 evenly.
6. Do the same with the 0.
7. Make a light shadow on the numbers. For more realism, shading and shadow can be rubbed with your finger.
8. Carefully trace the bottom layer under the number 2 with a pencil.
9. Also neatly draw out the bottom layer of the 0.
10. With a cotton swab, very gently rub the bottom layer to create a realistic shadow.
11. It's possible to go over the bottom layer with stroke likes and again rub the cotton swab to make the shadow darker and more uniform.
12. Position the picture approximately at the same angle. Done!

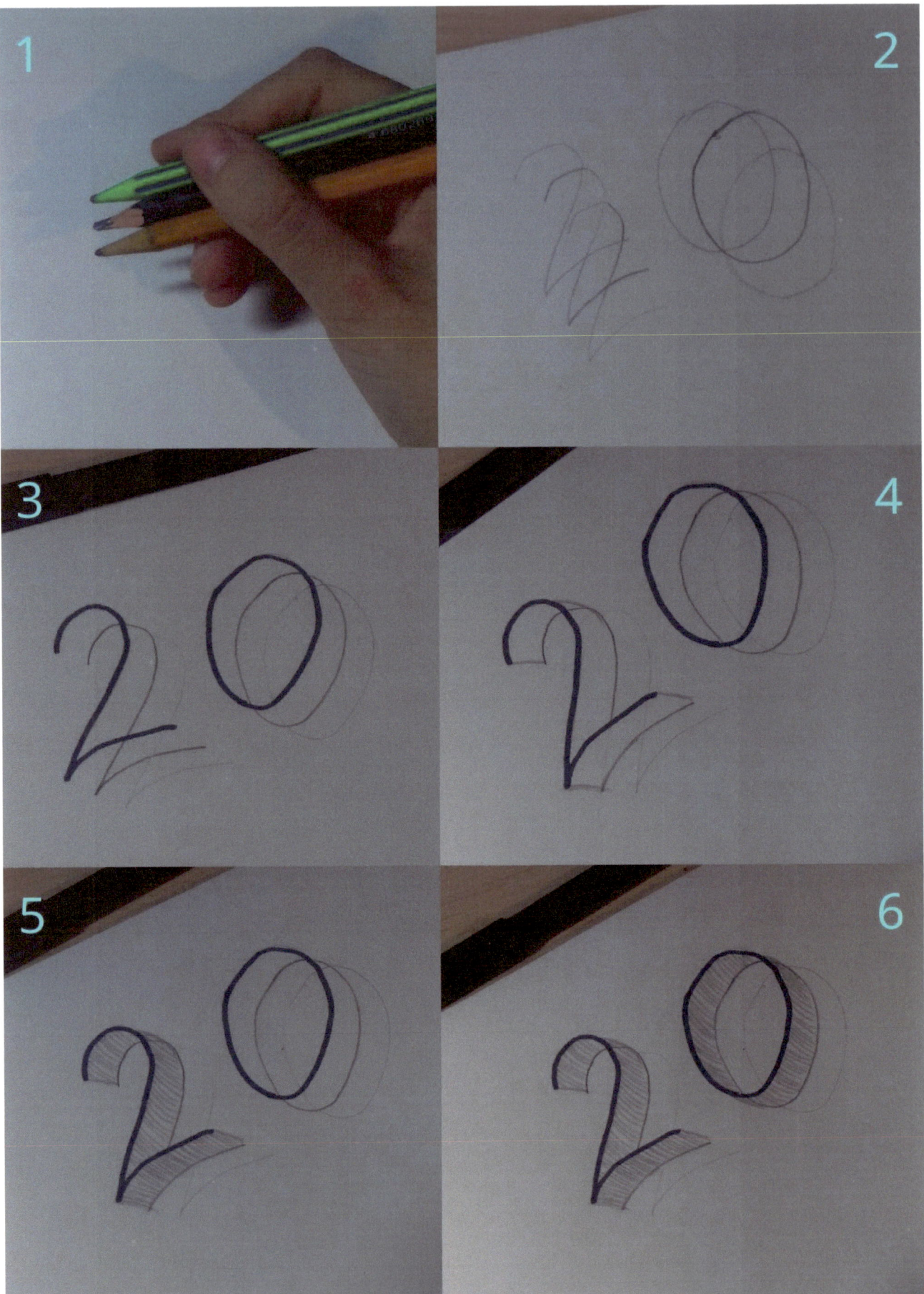

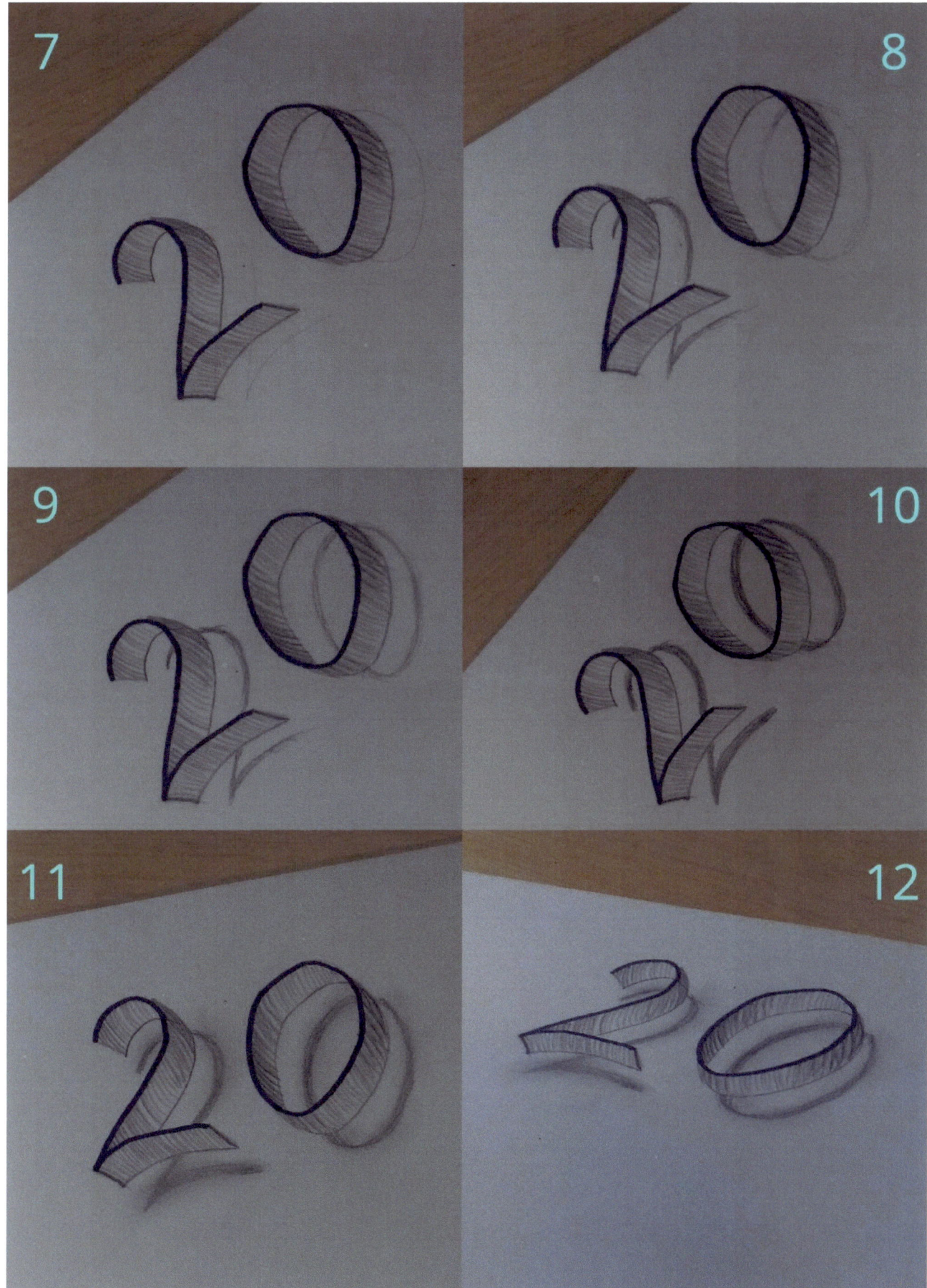

FLYING HEART

1. Using a pencil, draw 2 of the same rectangles on a sheet of paper, as in the photograph. Measure from the center of the top line a little less than an inch to the right and left; these will be the centers of the circles. Try to draw 2 identical circles.

2. From the outside of the circles, draw 2 lines to the center of the bottom line. This allows us to make the heart more symmetrical.

3. Erase excess lines, leaving only the heart.

4. Shade the pattern with curved lines. Leave some places unshaded; these are glare.

5. Make a shadow under the heart. The farther from the center, the bright the shade becomes.

6. Cut out the undesired paper just above the middle of the heart.

7. Slightly move the drawing away and lower your head. Choose the best angle. Done!

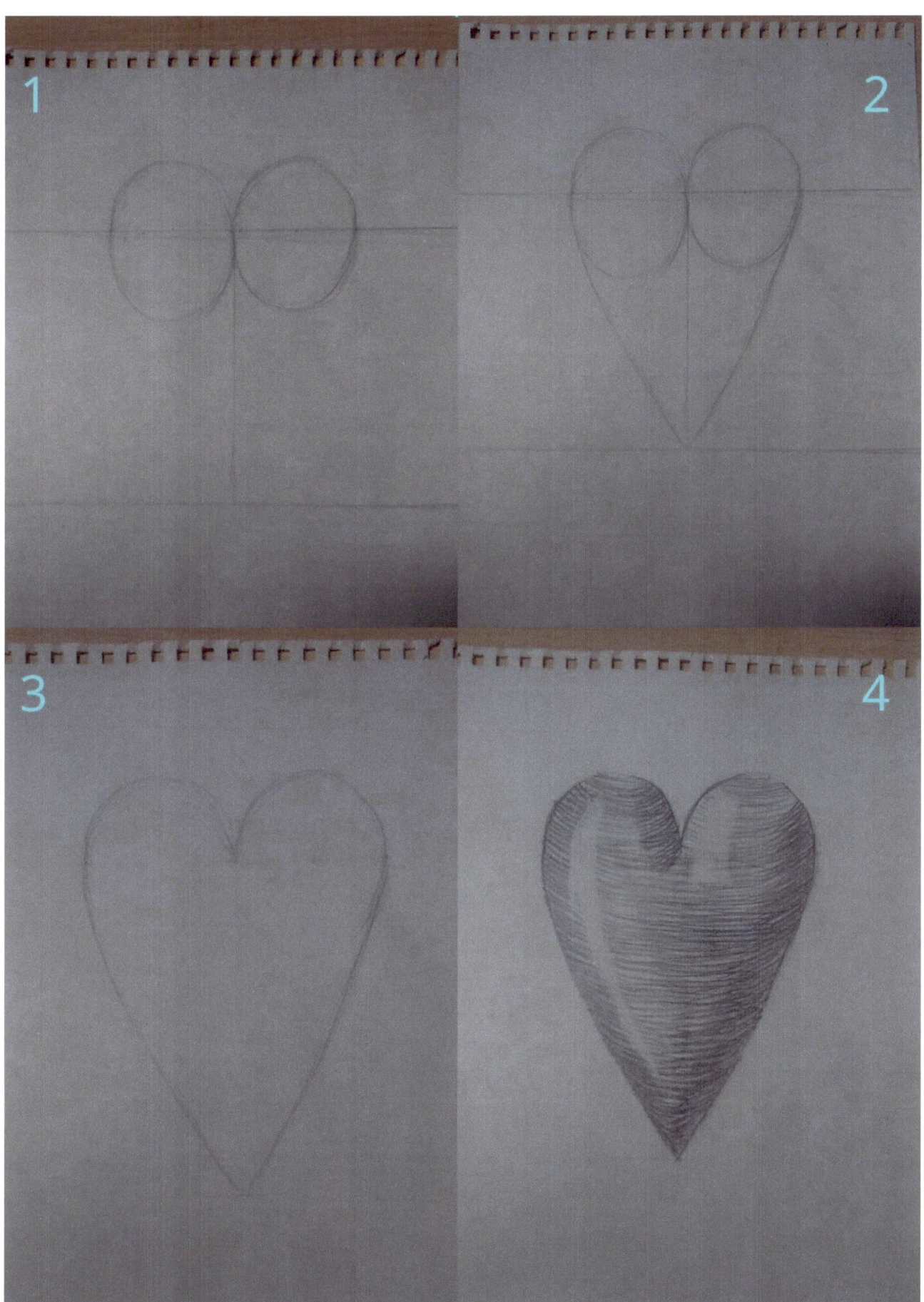

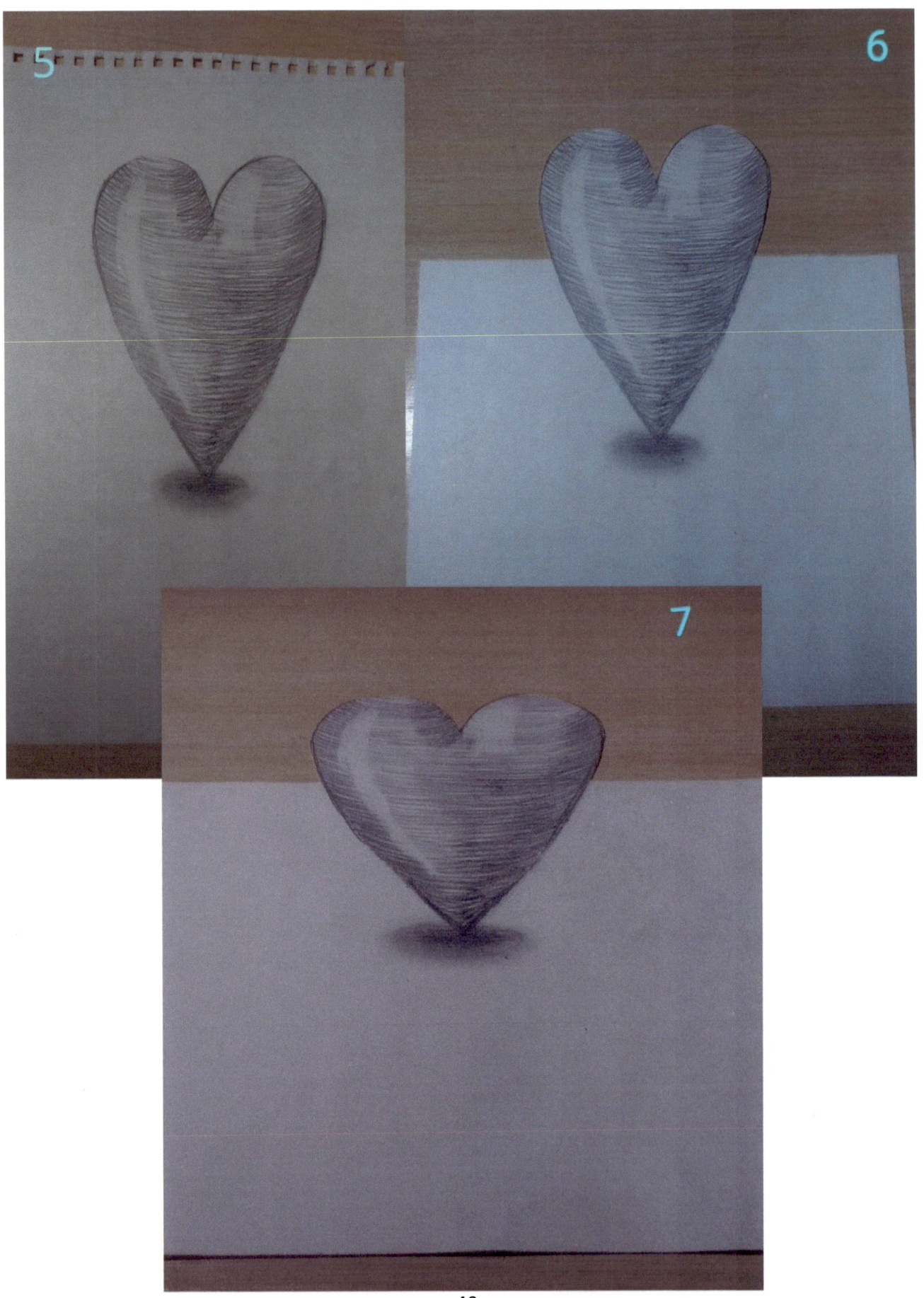

MORE FROM SOPHIA WILLIAMS

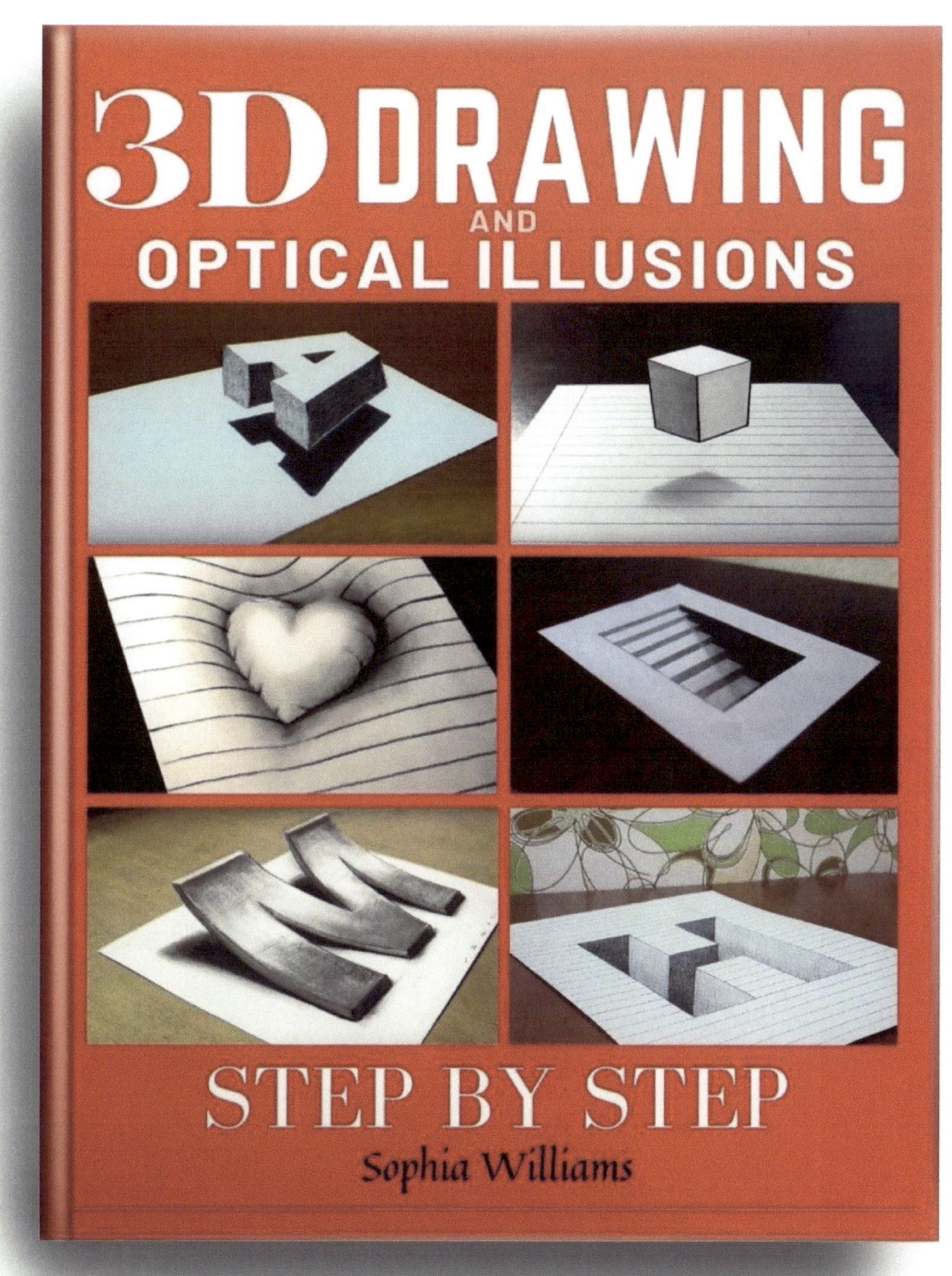

www.ingramcontent.com/pod-product-compliance
Lightning Source LLC
Chambersburg PA
CBHW040419220526
45473CB00004B/1291